Essential Skills for your Growly but Brilliant Family Dog

Books 1-3

Beverley Courtney

Books by the author

Essential Skills for a Brilliant Family Dog

Book 1 Calm Down! *Step-by-Step to a Calm, Relaxed, and Brilliant Family Dog*
Book 2 Leave it! *How to teach Amazing Impulse Control to your Brilliant Family Dog*
Book 3 Let's Go! *Enjoy Companionable Walks with your Brilliant Family Dog*
Book 4 Here Boy! *Step-by-step to a Stunning Recall from your Brilliant Family Dog*

Essential Skills for your *Growly* but Brilliant Family Dog

Book 1 **Why is my Dog so Growly?** *Teach your fearful, aggressive, or reactive dog confidence through understanding*
Book 2 **Change for your Growly Dog!** *Action steps to build confidence in your fearful, aggressive, or reactive dog*
Book 3 **Calm walks with your Growly Dog** *Strategies and techniques for your fearful, aggressive, or reactive dog*

Your free book is waiting for you!

Impulse Control is particularly valuable for the reactive and anxious dog. Get a head start with your training by developing astonishing self-control in your dog! Change your dog from quick on the trigger, to thoughtful and reflective.

Go now and get your step-by-step book absolutely free at
Brilliant Family Dog
www.brilliantfamilydog.com/freebook-growly

Disclaimer

I have made every effort to make my teachings crystal clear, but we're dealing with live animals here (that's you, and your dog) and I can't see whether you're doing it exactly right. I am unable to guarantee success, as it depends entirely on the person utilising the training programs, strategies, tools, and resources.

What I do know is that this system works!

Nothing in these books should upset or worry your dog in any way, but if your dog has bitten or you fear he may bite, you should take action straight away:

1. Use a muzzle
2. Consult a specialist force-free trainer

"I am not a vet"

You'll see this statement dotted about the book. I am not a vet, but there are some things with a medical slant that I need to draw your attention to.

I do not wish to wake up one morning and find my front lawn covered with angry vets brandishing syringes and latex gloves. On medical matters, take your vet's advice. You may want to seek out a veterinary behaviourist who specialises in this area.

Any opinions I express are based on my best efforts to study the literature, from personal experience, and from case studies. Not gospel, in other words.

Many of the techniques I show you were not invented by me, but I add my own spin. There will be a little repetition of key points from book to book, to ensure that the new reader has some understanding, and serve as a reminder to the rest of us. Ideally all three books should be read in sequence.

All the photos in this book are of "real" dogs – either my own, or those of students and readers (with their permission). So the reproduction quality is sometimes not the best. I have chosen the images carefully to illustrate the concepts – so we'll have to put up with some fuzziness.

Contents

Essential Skills for your *Growly* but
Brilliant Family Dog

Book 1

Why is my dog so growly?

Teach your fearful, aggressive, or reactive dog
confidence through understanding

Beverley Courtney

Introduction

Picture the scene: you're walking along the road with your dog when - horror of horrors! - another person with a dog appears at the end of the street.

You know what's about to happen.

You start to breathe faster, your heart rate speeds up, you clutch the lead tightly to you, keeping your dog's head close. By this time your dog is on full alert, wondering what on earth has frightened you so much.

And sure enough, it happens.

Your dog spots the other dog, and lunges forward on the lead, barking ferociously. You gasp out broken commands as you try to keep your feet on the pavement. You try to pin your dog against the wall as the other person marches by with their dog.

Did they just look down their nose at you? Did they shoot your dog a filthy look?

Now shame enters the mix. Your dog has behaved badly, you were quite unable to control him, and now you're condemned as a useless dog-owner with a nasty dog.

This walk has turned into a walk of shame and misery. Your dog is now on his toes, anxiously scanning for the next intruder to bark at. Your hands are sore, your throat is dry. You wish you could disappear into a hole in the ground.

Sound familiar?

The first thing to realise is that you are not alone!

There are lots of people who have dogs whom they love dearly - dogs who are a pleasure and delight about the house, calm, biddable, great with the kids. But as soon as they venture out of the door, the horns grow.

They seem to have a Jekyll and Hyde character - they're a house-angel, street-devil.

And you have tried everything and don't know what else to do.

Take heart! Help is at hand. I am going to help you to change things so that your dog will gain confidence, you will gain confidence, and walks will become an enjoyable pastime once more.

Why can I help you?

I, too, am one of those people with a dog who is wonderful at home - but outside was another story. Lacy's hackles would stand up like spines on a porcupine. She'd lunge and plunge, choking on her collar. She'd look for all the world as if she wanted to tear the other dog - or person - limb from limb. For all the dogs I've lived with, I'd never had this problem before.

What made this all so much worse was that I am a professional dog trainer! Someone who helps people get the best from their dog! Clearly I had a huge gap in my learning, and it was urgent that I plugged that gap as soon as possible. I needed to help my dog, and it was clear that there are plenty of other people out there wrestling with this largely misunderstood problem.

So I embarked on further studies. I devoured everything I could find that promoted a force-free approach to the problem. I already knew that the best way to interact with any animal (or person, for that matter) is by encouraging and rewarding the response you want, rather than demanding, commanding, and manipulating. I learnt why my dog was doing what she did, so I could reject anything that made life worse for her, or which debased my own humanity.

I could say my studies culminated with becoming a Certified Behavior Adjustment Training Instructor (CBATI), but that simply marked a stage in my learning. Every dog I work with has an individual history, an individual owner, and an individual personality. There's no one-size-fits-all. My learning deepens with each new dog.

Listening to these dogs' owners and studying the dogs themselves leads me to a bespoke training program for each one. And once you've read through these books you'll be able to choose what will work for you, and your dog - in your life.

Take care, though, if you are selecting strategies, not to throw out the baby with the bathwater! Try everything I offer you before making any decisions about what will or will not work in your case.

Solid results

It's important that you don't start blaming. "If only that dog hadn't attacked her," "That trainer taught me all wrong," "She had such a hard time in the shelter." What happened, happened. It's history. Start from where you are now and move forwards from there.

And my reactive dog? Lacy is 99% ok now, in any situation. She even comes to classes with me and acts as a demo dog. I know what will work for her, and when she's better staying home for the day. I'm always aware of how she perceives the world and its denizens, and I'm able to help her keep her cool and enjoy her life so much more - without asking too much of her.

You could write a whole book about each of the topics in these short books. Indeed those books have already been written, and you can find many in the Resources Section at the end of each book. If you like in-depth study, then go for it.

My plan is to give you a shortcut from where you are now with your dog to where you'd like to be - without having to buy a library of books and learn a new "language". Every trade and profession has its own jargon, and this can be very confusing, even daunting, for someone who just wants to know what to do!

I will work with you through the system that I have seen work time and again with many different clients and their very different dogs - in a surprisingly short space of time.

Look at what Scruffy's owners had to say:

> When we first contacted you for help with Scruffy, we were worried that we would have to put in place some extreme measures, or that we might not be able to alter his behaviour at all. In fact, his behaviour has greatly improved and this has happened much more quickly than we expected.
>
> Scruffy used to become frantic and scrape at the floor to get towards any dog he saw, even at a great distance. This was embarrassing and stressful.
>
> He is now able to look at other dogs and move away with us to continue his walk. *This is a massive improvement in just a few weeks.* It means that we no longer avoid dogs, but in fact go out looking for them so that we can work on his training. The tools you have given us have been simple to learn and easy to incorporate into our daily walks.
>
> We are all enjoying our walks a lot more than we used to, and are looking forward to continuing with the training and helping Scruffy to make even more progress. Thank you!

These three books stand alone, but are best consumed together, in order.

- The first tells you what's going on and why - and some of this may surprise you. It's essential to understand a problem before attempting to fix it. This section should bring you lots of "Aha!" moments.

- The second book goes into the detail of what you're going to change and how, what approaches will work best, and what you need to make it all work. Lots of Lessons in this section. And much of this will involve change for *you:* exciting!

- And the third gets you out there with your dog, enjoying a new way of walking and interacting with her, and making the scene at the start of this Introduction - mercifully! - a thing of the past. Lots more Lessons here, and Troubleshooting sections to cover all the "what ifs" you'll come up with.

My suggestion is to read through the book first so you know where you're going, then while your brain is filtering and processing this information, you can go back to the start and work through the Action Steps and Lessons with your dog.

For ease of reading, your dog is going to be a he or a she as the whim takes me. He and she will learn the exact same way and have similar responses. There will be just a few occasions when we're discussing only a male or a female, and that will be clear.

Now let's dive in, with a look at what on earth is going on with our dog.

Section 1

Reactivity - what is it?

Chapter 1

Sometimes Smidge's halo slips a little – but it's there!

What do we mean by this word "reactivity"? Basically, it means that your dog is reacting to his environment, but that instead of being able to assess the situation calmly, make good judgements, and move on, he's stuck in "See dog: bark!"

You may think your dog is weird - that one moment he's a happy dog inside the house, and as soon as you step outside he turns into a snarly monster. Imagine you're enjoying tea and cake at a friend's house. You're happy and relaxed. Then your friend takes you to see his reptile collection (Oh no!! Exactly what makes your skin crawl!). In that room full of snakes and lizards, do you feel as comfortable as you were in the tea-and-cake room? And when he opens the cage and offers you one to hold … that's when you may panic and need to get out of the room.

Have you ever felt anxious and jittery for some reason? Worried about an interview, perhaps, or waiting for news from the hospital. Every bang or squeak makes you jump! Imagine living in that state all the time.

And at the bottom of this is usually FEAR. The reason your dog is making such a hullabaloo at the sight of another dog (or person, bike, jogger, car, plastic bag, you-name-it) is because she's trying to keep it away from her. Putting on an Oscar-winning display of teeth, claws, and noise usually does the trick.

The other person or dog may think, "This is a nasty dog, I'm outa here," or you - in your embarrassment and confusion - take the dog away, or dive into someone's driveway till the other has passed. Either way, for your dog, the barking and lunging worked! The threat is no longer there!

Sometimes this response is totally misunderstood by the owner, who says, "He drags me towards every dog because he wants to play".

In a little while we'll be looking in detail at Dog Body Language. It's possible you are not recognising some of the things your dog is telling you! It will be much clearer when you've learnt his sophisticated method of communication.

Dogs do what works

I will be saying this over and over again. Your dog doesn't have a secret agenda to terrify the neighbourhood; she has no wish to fight with every dog she sees. All she wants is for the thing that's coming at her to go away. And she's discovered that her fear reaction of barking and prancing often works. So that's what she'll keep doing.

Until ... we show her another way to get the same result! Without anxiety, distress, and disarray.

Imagine a bunch of youths at each end of a street, hurling abuse at each other. They don't really want to close the gap and risk getting hurt! They just want to appear big enough to deter the other crowd from advancing towards them. The guy who is being restrained by his mates as he lunges towards someone - he often doesn't want to go through with his threat. If his mates let go he would have to find a way to leave without losing face.

Your dog is not aggressive, nasty, vicious - any of the names that passers-by may give her. She's just afraid.

If this comes as a surprise to you, have a look at other aspects of your dog - around the house for instance. Does she jump at loud bangs? Does she bark at visitors? Is she deeply suspicious of any new object in her environment, creeping up slowly to inspect it on tippy-toes with outstretched neck? Does she get distressed when she's left alone? Is it hard to brush her, or trim her feet?

All these can also be indicators of an anxious dog who is more likely to react to strange dogs, people, or things, when out.

And keep in mind that your dog can be afraid of anything at all. While many reactive dogs are reactive to other dogs, there are plenty who are just fine with other dogs, but terrified of traffic, or tractors, or people, or children …

But my dog's friendly!

Another reason some dogs become reactive is frustration. They may really want to meet every dog or person in the world and expect a good outcome. This may work when they're off-lead and able to get away (more about that later on), but it may also come apart quite quickly when the other dog doesn't welcome the intrusion, or is much bigger and bolder than your dog first thought.

Off-lead this can result in a panic response where your dog snaps and barks before running away. There is scope for this to go badly wrong, if the other dog joins in the fray. On-lead the frustration grows very quickly, as the dog does not have the freedom to do what he wants, and little impulse control to deal with these feelings. So he barks and lunges towards the other dog.

The symptoms are the same as for the fear-barker - though the underlying cause is slightly different. This dog's actions are often misunderstood by his owner, who fears they have an aggressive dog.

The frustrated dog may have poor social skills, racing up to a strange dog and hurling himself in their face, or on top of them. Imagine someone doing that to you in the street: you'd have a thing or two to say, I'm sure!

He may be stuck in puppyhood, thinking that racing up to every dog is ok. This dog needs to learn manners, just as our children do. We wouldn't accept behaviour from a teenager or adult that we'd accept from a three-year-old child. It would be most inappropriate. And yet many owners think it's ok that their dog should jump up at every dog they see, just because they think he's friendly.

Jekyll on-lead, Hyde off-lead?

I find a lot of people saying to me that their dog is only reactive on-lead, and that off-lead "he's fine!"

I can only say that I've never seen a dog-reactive dog who is "fine" off-lead.

A little study of dog body language will reveal a lot of signs of discomfort in this dog. The only advantage of being off-lead is that the dog can get away before things get out of hand. And because this is not possible when he's on-lead, we get the "fight or flight" result: b-a-r-k-i-n-g.

In this chapter we have learnt that

- Dogs who bark and lunge at other dogs are not necessarily aggressive
- Over-friendly dogs need to learn polite dog manners
- We may need to view our own dogs differently

Chapter 2

More factors in your dog's reactivity

While the main reasons for your dog kicking up are fear, fear, fear, and frustration, there are other contributory factors that make it more likely, that need to be approached.

A guardy nature

First of these is the guardiness of your dog. Many types of dog have been bred for generations to guard - property, people, flocks. One of the characteristics of their ability to be a good and effective guard dog is that they immediately notice anything that is out of place. A coyote on the horizon? A person who should not be there? A paper bag which should definitely not be there - unrecognisable and alive as it moves and flutters in the breeze.

This is known as sensitivity to Sudden Environmental Change (SEC), and you can see how it is a laudable trait in a dog you want for guard duty. But many people admire these dogs - typically, German Shepherd Dogs, all-purpose farm dogs like Kelpies and some Collies, flock guardians such as Pyrenean Mountain Dogs and Maremmas, farm-bred terriers in every shape and form who are bred to despatch vermin - and assume that the inherited traits and instinctive drives that made them what they are will evaporate once they are in their home as a pet.

Not so! They are part of the package. So we have to live with that or train new responses for our dog.

That's mine!

Any dog can be a resource guarder - it's not dependent on breed or type. It simply means that once they have something they value, they do not want to share it! This may be food, a bed, toys, tissues in the bin, balls in the park, or their greatest resource - their owner. Dogs who are reactive around their owner but not so bothered at a distance from them - or in their absence - are often thought to be protecting their owner. What they're actually protecting is their poor sorry selves. Their owner is the source of all good things in their universe, so no dog is going to get near!

Sometimes all it takes is for the owner to step away and take himself out of the picture for their dog to stop worrying about this. Such is the case with my resource-guardy mini poodle Coco, who can interact with new dogs far better when I'm not too close.

Resource guarding is something you need to address. The first essential is never to challenge a dog who is guarding something: you are likely to get bitten! This is not a case of the dog challenging your authority - he just has something he wants to keep! Teach him how to swap similar items - first low-value (to him) objects, then gradually working up till you can swap bones with him. Take things slowly and calmly. Let him think it out while you wait, holding out the new item for him to take as he drops the first. Say "Thank you!" as you pick up the dropped item, and hold it out for him to take again.

He'll soon learn that exchange is no robbery. When he appears with something in his mouth, you can extend your hand and ask (politely) to see it. Admire the item, reward him with a treat, and whenever possible give him back the item he gave you.

If your dog has already bitten while guarding something he values, you need to find a force-free trainer to work with straight away.

Associated complications

Further things that will often indicate a reactive dog (useful to observe when you have a puppy: reactivity often only shows itself during adolescence) are sensitivity to sound or touch, and separation anxiety.

Sound sensitivity

Very common in herding breeds, who are alert to the tiniest sound in the environment. Keep in mind that a dog's hearing is many times more sensitive than ours. Not only that, but they can hear things way out of our range.

There are plenty of dogs who come apart at the first firework. Once she knew what the sound meant, my Border Collie Tip would turn to jelly, tremble, and drool, as soon as she heard the "wheeeee" of a rocket going up. One of the benefits of her growing to the ripe old age of 15 meant that she had about three firework-free years as her hearing deteriorated with age!

You can work to desensitise your dog to the noise (more in a later chapter). Playing a sound recording at a volume so low that you can barely hear it is a good way to start. Gradually increase the volume as your dog shows she is still comfortable. I record firework displays on the tv at New Year and play them from time to time while we go about our normal business in the house. The sharp bangs and booms become an unremarkable experience.

Touch sensitivity

You'll find this in all sorts of dogs, notably in dogs who have been rescued. Touch has possibly become a bad thing for them. Street dogs may have had no experience of our touch in the critical socialisation and familiarisation period of very early puppyhood. Puppy farm (puppy mill) puppies will probably have had little touch stimulation from people. This as an experience all puppies should be introduced to early on.

19

A good way to do this is by counterconditioning and desensitisation (again - more in a later chapter). For now, use the Five Second Rule for touching a dog. If the dog wishes to interact with you, respond and touch, ruffle and chat, up to the count of five. Then move your hands, body, and face away. Your dog may want more, and nuzzle you to carry on your fussing. You can give another five seconds before pausing again. By the same token, if *you've* had enough, your dog should respect your turning away by stopping pestering you.

But your dog may surprise you, and give a quick shake and move away as soon as you stop. He's had enough! Quite revealing if it was your children doing the touching and counting. I'm not suggesting your children are doing bad things - just that your dog may be a bit wary of them and their unpredictability.

If your dog is over-sensitive to touch, be sure that any visitors know this routine. Known visitors should count up to only three seconds before releasing. Strangers, zero seconds.

An abnormally aggressive response to touch, especially in a sleeping dog, needs a thorough vet check for pain or other neurological cause.

Separation anxiety

It's been shown from studies that many dogs suffer a measure of anxiety when left alone. This can range from some discomfort all the way up to the mega-symptoms of endless howling, loss of bladder and bowel control, shredding anything they can get their teeth into - especially doors and doorframes - sometimes injuring themselves in their desperate attempts to escape.

Clearly, if your dog is showing these extreme symptoms, you need to deal with this straight away. Get help from a qualified force-free behaviourist, a veterinary behaviourist, or at the very least from a well-researched book (see Resources Section).

For lesser signs of agitation when you leave, start from puppyhood with crate-training or some other kind of barrier training. See the Resources Section for my book *Calm Down! Step-by-Step to a Calm, Relaxed, and Brilliant Family Dog*, the first book in the series **Essential Skills for a Brilliant Family Dog**.

Teach your pup how to relax at will, and be sure to give her things to chew while she nods off. Classical music (that's Mozart, Haydn and the like) has been proven to help dogs relax, so leave a suitable recording or radio station playing. A solid sleep routine is vital. And most importantly, practice leaving the pup for short periods right from the start, even if you stay in the house.

Not sure what your dog does when you're out? Leave a laptop or smartphone recording, then you'll know!

Even a small amount of separation anxiety is going to add up to a lot of stress for your dog. And to get the happy, carefree dog we all want means we have to eliminate as much stress as possible for him - in every part of his life.

Lack of impulse control

We all need impulse control. Your young child is able to leave the cakes on the table alone in the knowledge that he'll get some later on. Picture an adult with no impulse control. They're probably in jail.

Our dogs can learn impulse control just the same as we can. My dogs will leave those cakes on the table - even a nose-level coffee table - when I'm out of the room. This is a case of *what you expect is what you get*. I expect a lot of my dogs - but I do take the time to teach them first! They don't come with all this pre-installed.

For a detailed program to teach your dog impulse control, see the second book in the series **Essential Skills for a Brilliant Family Dog** - *Leave it! How to teach Amazing Impulse Control to your Brilliant Family Dog* (see Resources Section).

The skills involved will teach your dog to be reflective and thoughtful, instead of diving in gung-ho. These skills are essential to success in other parts of his life that he finds challenging.

ACTION STEP 1:

Acknowledge that it's not your dog's fault that she does what she does when out. You have a good dog - she just has problems in certain areas of her life. No need to blame her, her history, you, or anyone else. It just is.

But we're going to change it!

In this Chapter we have learnt that:

- Some dogs are more likely to be reactive than others
- They may be a victim of their heredity
- We need to treat the problem holistically
- Teaching calm and impulse control are essential
- Your dog needs help, not chiding

Section 2

Why did it start?

Chapter 3

The early days

Two pups meet freely on a Good for Dogs Puppy Walk

A lot of new puppy-owners are now aware of the importance of early socialisation. But many people think that it just means their puppy has to meet lots of dogs. While calm viewings and greetings and, where appropriate, play are indeed very important, there's a lot more to it than that. Socialisation, Familiarisation, and Habituation, should all go together.

That's to say, in their first 14 weeks of life puppies need to experience everything we expect them to live with in our world.

This will include dogs, cats, people, old people, children, washing machines, bikes, people arguing, cars, sheep, plastic sacks, waterways, hang-gliders, people with hats, dropped saucepans, stairs, shops, gravel paths, and so on. Everything they're going to encounter in normal life.

And while a lot of people have some idea that it's important, many of them sadly get it wrong, usually by leaving it far too late.

It should start with an excellent breeder who provides early enrichment in the puppies' environment, with objects, sounds, different textures, tastes, visitors, phones ringing, for example.

Even puppies with this good start can get lost along the way if fear of disease has them kept in the house till after 14 weeks. Fortunately more vets are understanding the importance of these early days, and recommend getting the pup out and about everywhere from Day 1 in your home – at about 8 weeks of age. (You can carry him.)

Socialisation and new experiences continue, of course, all the dog's life. The more novelty your dog encounters, the more he's likely to accept new things. These days dogs are kept indoors a lot more, separate from other dogs. In days gone by - and no doubt in some rural areas still - dogs were let out in the morning to wander where they wished. This is no longer safe or possible, and sadly we have lost a lot which contributed to the bombproof neighbourhood dogs of yesteryear.

As an example, I find that rescued street dogs tend to be great with other dogs, and afraid of people. This reflects their early life. They have learnt dog social skills and body language very well, which is why they survived. People perhaps represented danger.

Maturing, adolescence

Just like human teenagers, canine teenagers (approximately 6-14 months, depending on breed and size) go through a huge amount of hormone-driven change. They will get braver and venture further from their owner when out.

(This is also the time when your recall will break down, if you've just been relying on your puppy's infant clinginess to keep him coming back to you.) Some of this bravery may result in poor experiences. They may look almost full-grown, but the young dog's brain is still learning and changing.

One thing that can adversely affect this maturing process is early neutering - indeed neutering at any age can have undesired side-effects (see the Resources Section for info on the many scientific studies). By early I mean anything up to about 12 months.

We'll look at this in detail in Chapter 11. For now, hold off on the neutering plans.

Your dog's breed or type

We looked at the effect this can have on a tendency toward reactivity in Chapter 2, and found that guard breeds, guardian breeds, herding breeds, and terriers, were more likely to become reactive to novelty in their environment.

There's also a proclivity with some breeds to noise sensitivity and touch sensitivity. Anything that puts dogs into a heightened sense of awareness or adds stress to their lives is likely to erupt in the fear behaviour we've talked about.

Another aspect of this is that the friendly neighbourhood mutt that many of us grew up with – so suited to being a family pet - is being forced into extinction.

This is partly because of the aggressive neutering policies espoused by some cultures. The friendly neighbourhood breeding stock has been wiped out.

And the rise in consumerism has spilled over into dog ownership too, with its emphasis on having the latest, the best, the most fashionable - of everything.

It would make no sense for me to get a performance sports car: I drive at reasonable speeds, and need lots of space to carry family, dogs, and all their gear.

By the same token, it's not appropriate for many normal family households to take in a high-performance dog, which for generations has been bred for - tramping the moors eight hours a day; hurtling over or through any obstacles in their path to fetch and drive sheep; hunting down and killing anything small and furry; or patrolling properties all night on the lookout for ne'er-do-wells and intruders.

This is a placing which is not going to work!

Choosing a dog by its looks alone, without considering the purpose which has produced those looks, as well as the dog's needs and energy and stamina levels, is doomed to disappointment.

In this chapter we have learnt that:

- Outside factors can affect a dog's likelihood to become reactive
- It's possible to minimise these effects
- Choose "horses for courses"

Chapter 4

Medical causes

Clearly, a medical condition can affect your dog's character. There could be hidden pain that will naturally be stressful, tiring, and would put anyone on a short fuse!

I am not a vet, but I'm aware that there are also conditions which have been shown to affect a dog's worldview.

ACTION STEP 2:

Before embarking on any program of training or behaviour modification, you need to establish that your dog is sound. It's possible that some kind of medication will make a big difference, mentally or physically. So a thorough vet check (not just a quick once-over) is indicated. If you know your dog is experiencing pain or lameness, you can have a session with a qualified canine massage therapist, who are very good at uncovering slight or intermittent sensitivities. (This isn't snake-oil - it's a proper, recognised qualification!)

Personal history

Your dog may have been fine with other dogs up until the day he was attacked, let's say by a black terrier. Now he is (with some justification) afraid of all terriers, or all black dogs, or all male dogs, or all dogs.

Maybe your dog came from a shelter. You may know his previous history or you may not. Clearly it was not good, or he wouldn't have ended up in the shelter. Even if he was much loved by someone who has died, this is a scarring experience. For some dogs, a shelter is a 24/7 nightmare. I'm not blaming the hardworking and dedicated shelter staff here: for me, being transported to a holiday camp would be a nightmare!

Maybe the staff say he was "fine" with other dogs. Maybe he was. Maybe he was shut down and "keeping a low profile" (as I would, at that holiday camp!). The true dog was not apparent. It can take a dog at least eight weeks to settle into a new home and feel fully relaxed there.

If you went to live in someone else's home, you would start off being super-polite and considerate. "Where does this cup go?" "Is it alright if I sit here?" and such like. But after a few weeks, you'd be leaving cups on the floor, putting your feet on the furniture, and generally making yourself feel at home. So it is with your dog. Once he's truly relaxed and knows he belongs (that's a good thing!) he'll start to show sides of his character you didn't know existed (and that's fun!).

Copycats

If you are already blessed with a reactive dog, and you introduce a new dog into your household, take care not to take them out together until you're sure that your new dog is ok in the outside world. This reactivity is highly catching! And you may find you have not just two dogs barking (even if one's only doing it for the hell of it) but one may "redirect" a bite onto the other. Or you. That means because they can't reach the dog or person they want to frighten off, they grab the nearest thing, which could be your hand or thigh.

> ACTION STEP 3:
>
> If you get a new dog or puppy, rear it largely separately from your other dog. This is normal good practice in order to prevent your new pup becoming totally dog-focussed, and to give your older dog a break. If your older dog is reactive, then no group walks until your puppy is maybe a year old.

Fence running and window barking

Fence running (racing up and down inside your fence, barking at passing dogs, or the dog next door) and window barking (perching inside the window and alerting to anything that moves) are bad habits you don't want any dog getting into.

But for the reactive dog it's even worse. Being on guard duty all day long when he should be resting and sleeping is exhausting. And all this guarding behind a safe barrier gives a false confidence - a kind of Dutch courage from the heady repetition. When this dog is out and sees a dog, he thinks "Gulp! This one's not behind a fence or a window - now I'm in trouble!" and lets loose with his full panoply of barking, lunging and terrorising.

Remedies for window barking can be found in the free e-course at www.brilliantfamilydog.com For fence running you can employ similar strategies, only outside. The first of these is never leave your dog alone in the garden or yard.

If you don't want something to happen, you must make sure it can't happen.

In this chapter we have learnt that

- There may be hidden causes for your dog's behaviour
- You must ensure your dog is in the full of his health
- There are four things that can make it all worse!

Section 3

Why did it get worse, when I'm trying my best?

Chapter 5

It will get worse - unless dealt with

There are some things that dogs do that will go away on their own. Some puppy behaviours, like chewing, submission-weeing, digging, will simply evaporate if carefully managed. But there are other things - usually the things we really don't want! - that will build and build, getting worse and worse, until we decide to do something about it.

When we do something for the first time, a neural pathway in the brain is built. To begin with this pathway is fairly narrow and hard to find. Think, learning to drive a car - it's all foreign to us and hard to remember the sequences. But the more we repeat that thing, the wider and brighter the neural pathway becomes until we can just slide down it without a thought. It becomes our go-to response. We can drive on auto-pilot!

So every time your dog does something, he's building those neural pathways bigger and stronger. He doesn't have to think hard, as the learner-driver would to locate which pedal to press. It becomes his automatic, instant, response. In the case of our reactive dog: "See dog: bark!"

While this all started as a fear response, it's now become a habit as well. So while we change the fear response, we will also be teaching new and better habits.

It works for the dog

If there's something that's frightening you, your first instinct is to get away from it. If you can't get away from *it*, you'll try to get *it* away from *you*. Hence some manic responses to a wasp in the house!

When your dog puts on a song and dance routine of barking, whining, lunging, and prancing, at the sight of another dog, he's trying to get it to go away.

And this often works!

Either

- the other dog is frightened off and moves away
- the other dog's owner thinks "this is a nasty dog" and turns away, OR
- the barking dog's owner is shamed into beating a hasty retreat

If it works, he'll keep doing it. *Because he has no other course of action to rely on.*

Fight or flight

This well-known expression really comes into its own with the reactive dog. It's the reason many people think their dog is "fine" off-lead, but turns into a monster on-lead. As we saw in Chapter 1, this dog is usually not as "fine" as people think. It's only because the off-lead dog has the freedom to move away (*flight*) that things don't go badly wrong.

Once your dog is tethered to you, however, he knows he can't flee, so this leaves only *fight*. This can all be made worse by the fact that he's unable to express his body language and calming signals. It's difficult to look nonchalant and relaxed if your head is being held up in the air.

Trapped in a tunnel!

This feeling of being restrained or trapped can also be made worse by being in a "tunnel". This is the stuff of nightmares for many people: ahead is an all-consuming fire, behind is a crush of people and cars - panic!

For your dog this tunnel could be made up of walls and hedges and parked cars, as on a street pavement, or can be a real tunnel of a narrow footpath with walls and trees either side. Even being 10 yards from a field barrier - trees, or a hedge - can prompt the *fight* reflex, as the *flight* option is limited.

And what does the owner bring to this party?

Sadly, we often make this all far, far worse.

I know we don't want to, and we think we're doing everything we can to stop it. But we do tend to add fuel to the fire.

If you're like 99% of reactive dog owners, you'll be in a continuous state of shock and apprehension when out with your dog - just waiting for something to kick off. So you wind the lead round your hand a few times, just to be sure, to be sure. You keep your dog on a tight lead, close to you - as if creeping through enemy territory and waiting for mines to start exploding any moment.

And the second you spot another dog - BANG! Off goes the first mine. You gasp and breathe in sharply, you go trembly and flustery, you tighten that lead even further, gripping it to your chest. "Oh no!" says your dog, "What's she so afraid of? What have I got to bark at?"

Your understandable fear and anxiety over your dog is now triggering your dog's outburst.

A loose cannon

It may be that, up to now, you've really had little understanding of *why* your dog behaves as she does. You know all too well *how* she behaves! It seems to you that she is unpredictable. She's lovely at home, so why does she put on this other persona when out?

You've come to distrust your friend.

And this feeling of unease, distrust, panic, seeps into even the calmest of walks. Your dog is now on her toes! If *you're* afraid, then there must be something bad out there. Your dog will work hard to locate it and try and keep it away.

How stressful a pleasant walk with your dog has become!

This is no fun for either of you, and this is what we are going to change. But wait, there's more you need to know first.

A social pariah

Maybe you've found that the only way out of this nightmare is to walk your dog at 5 in the morning, or at dead of night - at The Hour of the Difficult Dog. The only people you see are other owners of difficult dogs, who will scurry away like rats in the sunlight as soon as they spot you.

You have now become a social pariah. When you first got your dog, you had happy visions of companionable walks with friends and their dogs. What has happened? Walks have now become a chore. There's no fun here for either you or your dog.

You know that what you've been doing up to now is not working. So here's a complete turnaround for you - and you'll be quite amazed at the difference it will make!

ACTION STEP 4

As soon as you spot another dog,

1. Relax
2. Soften your hands on the lead, keeping it loose
3. Breathe out
4. Say cheerily to your dog, "Let's go!" while you turn and head the other direction.

I can hear your protests already! Just try it. We'll address problems and fallout later.

In this chapter we have learnt

- That hoping it will all go away will not work
- Why your dog is choosing this response
- Where instinct comes into it
- How we are unwittingly exacerbating the situation
- How a change in your mindset can make a big difference to your dog

Chapter 6

Previous training

If your dog came to you as a re-home, you'll have had no input into his previous training. But if you've owned your dog from a puppy, you are responsible for any previous training your dog has had.

Though maybe not entirely.

- You may have gone to your local dog training school in the hope of giving your puppy the very best start in life
- You could have followed a tv personality who everyone is talking about
- Perhaps you took the advice of other dogwalkers or family members

Sadly, you may have found the only training offered to you was aversive training. The type of punishment-based training that used to be meted out to children in days (happily) gone by. You may have found these ideas run contrary to how you like to bring up your children, or deal with co-workers, but you were assured that these teachers knew best and that it was different with animals, so you went along with it.

What damage may have been done!

Any kind of aversive training can have a devastating effect on a dog's confidence in his ability to cope, or show emotions. If a dog has been punished when he saw a dog approaching and was afraid of it, how's he now going to feel about approaching dogs? "CLEAR OFF before I get into trouble!" is his noisy answer.

If that punishment has been with the gruesomely mediaeval prong collar, a painful choke chain, or for true barbarism, an electric shock collar, his response is going to be stronger and faster.

You will have to work against a fear reaction born of real pain. I hope I don't need to tell you to ditch any of this equipment if it's in your house? We'll be looking at humane equipment later on.

But don't blame yourself. You did the best you could with the knowledge you had. We're starting with a clean slate now, so there's no time for regrets or "what if's".

Punishment tends to drive problems underground. The hungry child who is beaten for stealing will not stop stealing: he'll just make sure he's never caught again! His hunger and deprivation won't go away. In the same way, if you punish an emotional response in a dog you aren't addressing the problem, just suppressing the reaction. The problem is still very much there, but with lots more anxiety attached to it. "I was afraid of the other dog - now I'm afraid of my owner too!" is not going to help change your dog's state of mind.

And suppressed emotions can get bottled up until, one day, the cork is blown out of the bottle and everything comes out, in a massive over-reaction!

Many dogs find themselves punished for growling, for example.

Never punish a dog for growling!

"Punishing a dog for growling is like taking the batteries out of a smoke alarm." Very well put by dog trainer Nando Brown. If your dog is not allowed to tell you of his anxiety by a low rumble of discomfort, then he may skip that step and go straight to the next one up - snapping or biting.

Regard growling as information. Your dog is telling you something – that he is really not happy with the situation. So you need either to remove him from the pressure, or remove the pressure from him.

Punishment can have a lot of unintended fallout. Punishment may involve pain and fear. But it may be much milder - like forcing a frightened dog to be in a place with lots of screaming children. You may not have intended to punish that dog, but that's what happened, in effect. And the erosion of the dog's trust in you, as well as your evident annoyance, is burying that problem ever deeper in the dog's mind.

If you get fish-poisoning after a restaurant meal, not only are you never going to that restaurant again - maybe you'll never eat fish again! A rather extreme response to a single event. But understandable.

Stress

And while we're looking at making things worse, we cannot overlook stress. Stress causes reactions to be exaggerated. Stress causes us to snap. Likewise your dog. And there are some areas of your dog's life that are building stress that will really surprise you.

1. Too many walks

"What!" you squawk! "I thought I had to take my dog out for a walk every single day! I thought I was doing the right thing!" Well, like so much in life, that depends. It depends on how your dog is experiencing these walks. A happy-go-lucky dog who loves meeting people and other dogs will relish his daily walks. But that's not the dog you have, or you wouldn't be reading this book.

It may be that your dog gets sick with anxiety at the very thought of a walk. The walk may consist of you getting upset or telling him off while he runs the gauntlet of narrow paths, fence-running dogs, squealing children, dog walkers walking their dog straight towards him, traffic noises, people wanting to pat his head …

This is not an enjoyable walk for an anxious, shy, or reactive dog!

There are two reasons for walking your dog. One is for exercise. The other is for socialisation. Clearly the second reason is a fail. So cut your losses, exercise your dog with vigorous play in the garden or on solo walks in a relatively dog-free zone - a forest trail, for instance - and save road walks for when your dog is calm and you can avoid most of the hazards.

We're focussing on the outcome here, guys - Calm walks with a happy and relaxed dog. If your daily walks are not a step in this direction, then you need to cut them right back.

2. Not enough sleep

Meggie and Marty hard at work

This one floors so many people! Adult dogs need to sleep 17 hours a day for mental and physical stability. 17 hours a day! Is your dog getting anywhere near 17 hours a day? If your dog paces and runs, chews and barks, jumps and dives, plays and chases all the time at home, he is not living the carefree life you may imagine! I have seen the dramatic improvements that result from getting this one right.

Teaching your dog how to relax, switch off, and get that urgently-needed restorative sleep will transform your dog's worldview. For a full guided program, check out *Calm Down! Step-by-step to a Calm, Relaxed and Brilliant Family Dog,* the first book in the series **Essential Skills for a Brilliant Family Dog.** It's free at all e-book stores, and you can find the details in the Resources Section.

Yawn …

3. Stress in the home

Your home may be a wonderful, sunny, joyful place of love and harmony. But your dog can still get stressed there! There may be anxiety when she's left alone. There could be rumbling disagreements with another family pet. The new puppy is driving her nuts and won't leave her alone. There could be so much noise and activity from the children and their school friends, that your dog can't get a moment's peace. Maybe you have a thieving problem with your dog which causes some friction. Perhaps she barks at the window, annoyingly.

Solutions to these problems can be found referenced in the Resources Section. The thieving, for instance, can be resolved, painlessly, by the second book in the series **Essential Skills for a Brilliant Family Dog**: *Leave it! How to teach Amazing Impulse Control to your Brilliant Family Dog.* And you'll find a free e-course for all those annoying habits your darling dog has developed.

4. Daycare or a dogwalker

A very perceptive reader sent me this query recently: "My question is, what do you think of daycare for dogs? Are the dogs actually happy about it, or do dog owners just like to imagine they are?"

I am not going to tar all daycares and dogwalkers with the same brush. But I will say that it's very hard to find a convenient one which is truly a safe place for your dog to learn and develop. Think of the skills you need as a parent to prevent open warfare in your own household! Then picture a gang of dogs being thrown together for a walk - or all day in a confined area - in the care of people who frequently have no dog training or behaviour qualifications whatever. "I love dogs" may help, but it's not a qualification. And given how long it takes us to learn how to care for our own species - and that a lot of what people think about dogs is wrong - you're going to be lucky to find somewhere safe for your dog.

I was recently shown a promotional video for a daycare by someone who's been sending her very reactive German Shepherd pup there for months. Even in this 30-second video - meant to show how wonderful the place was - I could see bullying and intimidation of this pup by other dogs, and no-one going to her aid. Imagine what this sensitive puppy is subjected to for ten hours a day, five days a week! No wonder her reactivity is already extreme at only six months of age. What the owner thought as "being perfectly happy at daycare" was in fact a dog that spent all day trying to avoid the other dogs (quite impossible with those numbers of loose dogs) - shut down, in other words. Not fine at all.

For many dogs, daycare is viewed with the same suspicion I view that holiday camp!

My personal solution to an enforced absence from home is to have someone I trust to come in to let the dogs out in the garden and play with them for a while during the day.

If anything goes wrong in a daycare or with a dogwalker, you will be paying for that for years - possibly the rest of your dog's life. Think hard, and do a lot of homework, before going for that option. Apart from checking out the daycare's mission statement for aversive practices, you could do well by asking to spend an hour just observing, or join the dogwalker for one of her walks.

In this chapter we've learnt that

- Old sins have long shadows
- Stress, the silent killer, can affect your dog even when you think you are doing the best for her

Chapter 7

Other factors that can make things worse

Diet

I am not a vet.

We all know how much diet affects our health, and we take care to ensure we're following government guidelines, and to minimise the junk our children get hold of. We also know the value of a varied diet of fresh foods, so that we get the greatest spread of nutrients.

So why do people chuck that all out of the window when feeding their dog?

Their dog has to put up with the same bag of food - often with a ridiculously long shelf life and sell-by date - year in, year out. No variation, no broad spread of nutrients, no fun.

Commercial dog food is big business! But sadly, choosing the bag with the cutest picture is not the way to get the best for your dog. A little online research will take you to a comparison site for dog foods for your part of the world. Look for a site written by a canine nutritionist, rather than a manufacturer. And take care that it is independent and in no way affiliated with the manufacturers it's putting at the top of the charts.

Clearly, what affects the body also affects the mind. You can't feel ready to face the world if your skin is poor or your joints aching. So the reactive dog needs special care in regard to food.

Here are some pointers for you:

1. If it's advertised widely and available in prime position at your local supermarket, you should probably avoid it.

2. If its first ingredients feature cereals (maize, corn, wheat, barley) you should definitely avoid it. Dogs are not chickens.

3. If it has named protein sources (e.g. lamb, beef, not "meat"), no chemical additives, and you can't see the word "derivative" in the list, it's probably a good bet.

4. Many people consider a raw diet of meaty bones, offal, fish, and egg, as the most suitable diet for a dog. You can get this in convenient frozen packs, but be sure to augment with fresh stuff from your local butcher.

5. Your dog's poo should be firm and small. Copious loose stools (in an otherwise healthy dog) can be an indicator of a poor diet, as the dog is not absorbing his food but sending it all straight through.

6. Commercial dog treats can be very poor quality. Make your own fresh ones! Very easy, and cheaper - I'll be covering that in these books.

7. Whatever you choose to feed, ring the changes! If you and I ate the exact same diet, one of us may get fat and be short of, say, iron, while the other may get thin and have an excess of iron. (You can tell I'm not a doctor either!) We are individuals.

You have to become a good stockman and feed for condition. Ignore the feeding quantities written on the pack, and keep a close eye or hand on your dog's body condition. You should be able to feel the ribs, but not cut yourself on them! You should be able to easily locate the pin bones at the top of the pelvis, and there should be no hard rolls of fat round the neck and shoulders. Your dog's walking should be smooth and fluent, not a swaying waddle.

Feeding the best diet you can afford for your dog (and the best feeds are by no means necessarily the most expensive) will save you a boatload of money in non-attendance at the vet. Your dog's teeth will be white and naturally clean, his skin and coat good, his joints well held together, his health at optimum level. That is what I have found in my own dogs.

ACTION STEP 5:

Check out dog foods (don't die of shock when you read the label on the one you're feeding!) and move your dog up to a better one. Some change in behaviour can often be seen in as little as two weeks. Change the food gradually over a few days to allow the gut to catch up to the new food.

Copying your other dog

As mentioned in Chapter 4, copying your older reactive dog can be disastrous. The two dogs give each other Dutch courage. And barking is very self-rewarding - fun!

So if you're struggling to walk the two of them together, make life easier for yourself and walk them separately most of the time. You may, for instance, take Dog A out for a roadwalk on-lead one morning, and Dog B the next. They can have joint walks when it's mostly free running, perhaps each day. But refer back to **Chapter 6: Stress** and be sure your fearful or anxious dog is not getting too many bad experiences on walks.

Solo walks give you time to enjoy each dog separately, and if your walks have been a battle wrestling with twisting leads and spinning, barking dogs, they'll restore the pleasure to your walks. Sometimes your reactive dog gets the lion's share of attention, so taking your calmer dog on walks alone with you is very valuable to build that bond. Remember, your younger dog can become very dependent on your older dog if they spend too much time together - with catastrophic results when you lose the older dog. It's important to foster an independent spirit in your younger dog.

Other owners

This is where things can get tricky and unpredictable. Being told you have a nasty dog when you are trying to untangle the lead from your legs and calm said dog down is less than helpful. Having another dog owner stand in front of you being snooty about their dog's good behaviour is *no help at all* when your dog is reacting to their proximity!

We feel a lot of social pressure to put up with things we don't like and not rock the boat. In this case you are your dog's sole protector. If you know your dog needs distance, then that's what you give her.

Don't mind what other people think. You may never see them again, and what do they know? If their dog is calm around other dogs, they have *no idea* what we have to cope with! I once heard someone on the radio, referencing the straitened circumstances of her early adult life, saying something like: "Nobody who has money and no children can know what it's like to have children and no money."

And I'll add that nobody who has a dog who can handle every situation can know what it's like to have a dog who is frightened of almost everything.

Know that - once you've absorbed all the precepts in this book - you are doing your best for your anxious dog, and you'll know by seeing the great changes that will take place. Don't worry about the know-it-alls!

.. and other dogs

There's always going to be a time when you have to cope with an incoming dog. And whether it's over-friendly or aggressive, it will have a similar effect on your dog.

There are various suggestions for what you can do. Some people, knowing that their dog is better off-lead - and obviously only if there's no road nearby - will unclip the lead and keep back, ready to call their dog out for a treat or toy if things are going downhill. Others suggest tossing a handful of treats towards the incomer.

I know that asking the owner to call their dog is a total waste of time. Why? Because they have zero recall and they're not about to demonstrate that to you!

Sometimes I've caught the incoming dog by the collar and waited for the owner to trudge the 100 yards or so to come and fetch him. You need to be feeling strong enough to face their ire if you try this. If your dog is very small, you can teach her to jump up into your arms. Her jumping up is safer than you bending down and putting your face between the incomer and your dog. If the dog is going to grab your dog, they may grab you too.

You can try turning and running away, but dogs run very fast! Whatever you do, don't use any kind of aversive gadget (like a spray or noise), which will affect your dog just as much as the other dog, and make things much worse next time it happens.

Fortunately, in my own experience, genuine dog-dog attacks are pretty rare. Usually it's all sound and fury signifying nothing. The dogs have good bite inhibition, in other words. Real, savage, attacks can happen as a result of a misplaced strong predatory drive, and for that reason I keep my small fluffy dog still or lifted up when blooded greyhounds are in the vicinity.

Later on, you'll be learning an Emergency Turn which is tremendously useful for getting your reactive dog to forget the incomer and bounce away with you. This normally causes the other dog's advance to fizzle out. I'll also be giving you lots of advice on coping with an incoming dog. Real help is on the way in the next book! But learning first what's going on and why things are happening is critical to your future success in changing your life.

In the next Section we are going to learn some key skills and strategies to get you going in the right direction. Towards calm, peaceful walks.

In this chapter, we have learnt that:

- What you're putting into your dog's mouth can greatly affect his mindset
- Other family dogs can make things worse
- Other people and their dogs can make things a lot worse!

Section 4

What can I do?

Chapter 8

Change

"NOW you're talking!"

We've taken a good look at what is up with our dog, what started it, and what made it worse and kept it going. Now we're going to look at what we can do about it.

The first thing is to change. Obviously, you want things to change. But a lot of this change is going to come from *you*. Without change we can't expect different results. They say that it's a sign of madness to keep doing the same thing and expect a different result!

You see it every day when someone in the park calls their dog - to whom they have not taught a recall. They stand and yell. And yell. And YELL. They get crosser and crosser and their dog still doesn't come. They need to change something or they can stand there all day calling. (Hint: if he won't come to you, go to him. And cut the yelling.)

So we need to change our mindset. This was hinted at in the Action Step for Chapter 2: *Acknowledge that it's not your dog's fault.* It's so easy to blame someone or something when things go wrong. Blame is counterproductive. It just gives people an outlet for their frustration without doing anything material to effect a change. I'm not suggesting you blame yourself either, though as you saw in Chapter 5, you most probably contributed to it.

So many times people say "Ah well, he's a rescue dog …" and this after having had the dog for five years! He may once have been a rescue dog, but after a rescue dog has been in my home for a few minutes he's now *my* dog, no longer a "rescue dog". Parents don't say, "These are our children, but that one's adopted." You'd be scandalised! Accept that this dog is now your dog, that what went before is out of your control, and that moving forward together things will change for the better. No need to wind back the clock and try and blame something that happened long ago. Start from where you are.

As you learn new ways to work with your reactive dog you'll grow in confidence and understanding. You'll begin to truly empathise with your dog. You'll understand her. And she'll love that and respond to it. You're in it together.

The training method that works

Whatever system, method, or vague idea you were working with before, you are now going to switch over to choice-based training. Why? Because it works! But seriously, it's been scientifically proven to work. That is to say there have been many experimental studies, using scientifically approved methods for testing parameters and data collection, which prove beyond doubt that it works. There isn't any argument.

There are still plenty of people, sadly, who don't hold with this science nonsense and think that bullying and intimidation is a better method. But we'll leave them to stew in their own juice while we move forward into the light and do the job properly.

I'm not going off on a rant about the horrors of punishment-based training. If you've come this far with me, you probably share a lot of my views already. Suffice to say that if you put yourself into the position of the dog who is being poked, shouted at, threatened, given electric shocks, swung in the air by the throat till they are suffocating (all established "training" techniques) you would not be feeling very well disposed to the world in general. Miserable, in fact. And ready to bite the next thing that comes near you.

So what is choice-based training?

This simply means that you accord your dog a measure of intelligence and autonomy, and involve him in decisions which affect him.

So instead of saying, "Do this," you'll be saying, "What should you do now?" And no, this is not a recipe for chaos. You teach your dog to think, to problem-solve, to work out what is the best action to take at any given time. Now, instead of having a dog you bark "commands" at and who largely disregards them ("Sit, stay, SIT, I said sit, come here, stay, sit, WILL you come here, stay, good boy, sit!" Sounds familiar? It's exactly what I heard someone saying to their dog this morning), you have a dog who anticipates the right action and offers a sit when it seems a good idea, and then stays sitting until released.

You build this up by the simple method of:

Reward what you like
Ignore what you don't like
Manage what you can't ignore

This is now your mantra! Recite it daily, and twice before breakfast.

Until you get going with some of the Action Steps coming, where the speed of learning may surprise you, you'll just have to believe me when I say that it's that simple! You'll have an engaged and active learner, you'll be doing nothing remotely nasty, and your dog will build an ever stronger bond with you.

I discovered early in my parenting career that framing things as a positive removed huge amounts of conflict from my day. So we had:

Not "No boots in the house"
but "Boots go outside"

Not "Don't come to the table in pyjamas"
but "Boys who are dressed get breakfast"

Not "No tv till you've done your homework"
but "Would you like to watch your programme then do homework, or homework first?"
(There was no offer of skipping homework.)

Not "No computer games"
but "Do twenty minutes typing training then you get to play twenty minutes games"

This one really paid off as both boys could touch-type very fast by age 12 - one of my early goals for them.

Honour the dog

This goes hand in hand with acknowledging that it's not your dog's fault. He has opinions and feelings himself, and by honouring those feelings you can show true empathy. Your dog is not an automaton, a toy for people to play with. He's a sentient being and has a right to be consulted, and his thoughts and feelings taken into account.

Your dog is not something you do things to. He's someone you do things with.

Diet

If you want an engine to function properly, you have to put in the right fuel. We know this for our car. We also know this for our family. Extend this to your dog! If you haven't already done so, follow Action Step 5 in Chapter 7 -

to thoroughly research feeding options for your dog, and make the necessary improvements.

Understanding

I hope that by now, having read the first part of this book, that you have a far greater understanding of what is going on with your dog. Knowing that he's not a bad dog, just a frightened one, will make a difference to how you manage him when out.

You can cope far better with the social pressures that afflict you when your dog is on his toes, ready to erupt at a passer-by, when you know that he's a good dog having difficulty. Dogs are not people, and we need to understand how the mind of another species works. I find that the more I learn about my dogs, the closer our bond becomes, and the more I marvel at the fact that the human race can live so harmoniously and mutually beneficially with another species. It is truly an honour to experience this.

I will be telling you a lot about how dogs think and do. You'll find this an area of continuing interest - the more you learn, the more you'll want to learn! Having said that, you do not have to be a scientist or a professional dog trainer to make the techniques work. You do need a measure of understanding - especially of the fallout of doing things the wrong way - so you can field all those "helpful suggestions" volunteered by people who have no expertise, and put them in the "Thank you, I'll bear that in mind" folder. (Then never open that folder again.)

Take pressure off the dog

Your first priority is always going to be to keep your dog calm. "Under threshold" as it's sometimes known - the threshold being the doorway from calm to lunatic. "What about keeping *me* calm?" you say! See this: if your dog is calm, you will be calm.

61

And yes! it can happen. Not only *can* it happen, but it *will* happen. You may have been promised the earth by a previous trainer, who used old-fashioned methods to intimidate the dog into different behaviour. Quite often, the dog behaves very well with that trainer, then reverts to type with you - because you're not prepared to pursue the methods used and inflict pain and suffering on your dog.

The methods I will be showing you are all entirely force-free, and involve the dog making good decisions. This is what will effect a genuine change in your dog - it's not inflicted from without, but grows from within.

You will have the pure joy of looking into your dog's eyes when a situation arises that would previously have sent him into a tailspin - and seeing reflected there the calm confidence you feel, and the appreciation he feels for you.

Your dog needs a stress-free zone to learn new ways of reacting before applying them in a stimulating situation. So your first change is going to be in where you take your dog.

You may have been advised to keep exposing your dog to her fears, either in the name of socialisation or as a training technique. As we saw earlier, true Socialisation only takes place between the ages of 3-14 weeks.

But experiencing new things should always involve good experiences, and the dog should be taken away from anything that she's not happy about. Imagine you were terrified of mice: would it help you to have to put your hand into a cage full of them? As they crawled over your arm and nibbled your fingernails, would this make you less afraid of them? Would it perhaps make you anxious about the "expert" who was making you do this? This technique is known as "flooding" and is discredited as a humane method of working with a dog. We'll look at this in more detail in Book 3, Chapter 1.

So the dog that's afraid of traffic is *not* forced to stand at a busy crossroads for an hour (yes, people do this). This way you'll end up with a dog that's more afraid of traffic than before! Now I'm sure you want to minimise the stress your dog is under, and not force him to tolerate situations which are frightening for him.

Having to spend hours in the close and inescapable proximity of other dogs, whether in a daycare or group dogwalking setup, group classes, or on walks in narrow confined spaces, such as streets and footpaths, is stressful for someone who fears dogs! So this is where you're going to make some changes.

I know some may be hard to implement. You may have to pay slightly more for a more personal dog-sitting service; you may have to get the car out and drive to suitable walk spaces; you may be sorry to have to leave the group classes that *you* enjoy. But our aim is at this stage to focus on your dog's wellbeing and state of mind. Nothing will change until we change that.

ACTION STEP 6:

Check out alternatives to daycare. Either a very small family group in a private home, or a minder who can visit during your absence. Your fearful dog does not need to be taken for a walk by someone else - especially someone who doesn't know this stuff.

ACTION STEP 7:

Change or quit training class. Classes should have no more than eight puppies or six dogs. They should be calm, and focussed on the individual dog and owner. No shouting. No punishment. No threatening or intimidation. The trainer should be professionally qualified and part of a force-free organisation (see Resources Section).

ACTION STEP 8:

First of all, if walks are miserable and tense, cut down the walks! Exercise your dog at home and venture out only to places which are safe for him. Seek out open spaces where you can see incomers for hundreds of yards all around you. Avoid narrow paths and "tunnels", and anything that makes your dog feel trapped.

ACTION STEP 9:

This step is critical! *Show your dog she never has to meet another dog or person ever again.* When you and your dog see something coming that you know will upset her, you say a cheery "Let's go!", turn, and head in another direction. Your reward will be the relief you see in her face.

In this chapter we have looked at some of the changes you will have to make:

- Your attitude to your dog and her problem
- Seeking out and understanding a new training approach
- Understanding your dog and empathising with her
- Changing some of your habits and current practices
- Avoidance

Chapter 9 Keep changing!

The Precious Name Game

Your dog's name should be precious. She should think that it always means something good - she should be in no doubt about that. If you've ever spoken to your dog in frustration (hands up, guys - which of us hasn't lost it on occasion?) as in "Flossie? Who did this?" or "Flossie-get-over-here-this-instant!", then you've set up a bit of conflict in your dog's mind about whether "Flossie" means undiluted fun and pleasure or an impending telling-off.

So you need to make a change here straight away! The answer is simple. You only use your dog's name when you can pair it with good things. And if you're ever frustrated or annoyed, you don't use her name. Watch out for other family members as well as yourself. You may be surprised at how much negativity is being attached to your dog's name on a daily basis!

Lesson 1
The Precious Name Game

Here's a simple game to get you started - the Precious Name Game:

- Say dog's name cheerily whenever you notice her
- When she responds - by raising an eyebrow or hurtling towards you and crashing into your legs - reward her with something good
- Repeat at every opportunity throughout the day
- Enjoy your dog

Your reward may be a treat, putting her lead on for a walk (if walks are enjoyable), opening the door to the garden, playing a game, and so on. We'll look at rewards in greater depth in the next book.

Collar hold

This is - maybe surprisingly - another relationship-builder. If your dog stands still for you to slip your hand in her collar, this indicates a measure of trust - especially if it's in a tricky situation where she's worried.

If your dog is young and playful, she may intercept an approaching hand with her mouth, in order to start a game. Not so good. And if your dog has recently been re-homed with you there may be a history of collar-grabbing, dragging, and hurting (remember, we're not going to go there and use it as an excuse) which makes her understandably uneasy about having her collar felt.

So we're going to teach anew that your hand in your dog's collar means only good things. You'll see it's similar to the Precious Name Game above.

Lesson 2
The Collar Hold

Here's how you do it:

1. Have a supply of scrummy treats to hand
2. Have one treat ready in one hand, and with the other hand reach out and touch the side of your dog's face - just for a second - then remove your hand, feed the treat
3. Repeat Step 2 until she's happy to let you touch her face
4. Repeat Step 2, but reach and touch the side of her neck - just for a second - then remove your hand, feed the treat
5. Repeat Step 4 till she's happy
6. Repeat Step 4, but touch the collar for a second before feeding the

treat

7. Keep going till you can slip a finger into her collar, remove your hand - feed treat
8. Eventually you'll be able to slide your hand softly into her collar, with the back of your hand resting against her neck, and walk a few steps with her beside you before feeding the treat
9. When you reach towards your dog's collar she'll stay still and allow you to hold it then stay with you

Watchpoints:

- This will take as long as it takes. Maybe one session of a couple of minutes, maybe ten sessions - doesn't matter
- Be sure to remove your touching hand before feeding the treat
- Work very fast - touch-remove-treat, touch-remove-treat, keep it light and fun
- You are never pulling on this collar, not even gripping it firmly
- The goal is to be able to slip your hand into your dog's collar whenever you need to

When your dog feels the back of your hand against her neck she will now relax and stay still beside you. This is a great calming strategy for a reactive or anxious dog.

ACTION STEP 10:

Practice both these new skills daily. Little and often, and only in a safe place where your dog is relaxed and comfortable (most of my training takes place spontaneously, for just a minute or two, in the kitchen). The very thought of these games should produce a happy tail-wag.

Lead Skills

"Lead skills? You just clip the lead on the dog and hang on tight, don't you?" If that's what you're thinking, even a little, I am about to open up a new world for you! A world where you communicate with your dog, give her confidence and courage, and allow her to be a dog - all through your lead. And as a spin-off, your shoulders will stay comfortable, and your walks more relaxed.

The key thing here is that once you've mastered these skills, *you will never have to pull your dog's lead again.* What joy!

With a reactive and unpredictable dog, you've probably been holding on pretty tight to that lead. You've maybe thought that you have to have close control the whole time or else your dog will cut loose and savage someone. I really do understand! I've been there myself.

But you'll be pleased to know that in fact the opposite is true. The more relaxed your hands are on the lead, the more relaxed your dog will be. You want to change your mindset from desperate control, to protecting and helping your dog.

The lead is there to keep your dog from running under a bus, and to help with her self-control when she sees something that worries her, and, most importantly, it's a connection between the two of you. Messages go up and down this lead. Keeping it tight with a vice-like grip will prevent any communication.

The Opposition Reflex

If you were standing next to me and I pulled your arm - you'd pull back. You have to, in order to stay upright. This is called the Opposition Reflex and stops us falling over all the time.

Your dog has the same reflex! So if you pull his collar, he's going to pull away from you, in order to stay upright. If your lead is really tight - so tight that your dog is straining into his collar and your hands and arms are aching as you pull back - and I come along with a pair of scissors and cut the lead in half, what's going to happen? You'll probably both fall over!

So let's stop this madness now and make life easier for both of you.

It takes two to tango, as the saying goes, and it takes two to have a tight lead.

One of us has to stop pulling, and as we're the ones with the bigger brains, it needs to be us. Sadly, this pulling has often started in puppyhood and is now an entrenched habit. When people have their cute new little puppy, they tend to let it pull them all over the place. They think it is kind.

It is not kind.

It's teaching the puppy to damage her throat and neck (you'll learn much more about this in the next book) and to ignore the person on the other end of the lead. Picture this: they have their pup on a lead. The puppy pulls towards something. Their arm stretches out. The puppy pulls harder. With outstretched arm they follow the puppy.

What has this puppy just learnt? "If I pull, they'll follow. And if I pull harder, they'll follow faster!"

For some reason that escapes me, people find this appealing. Once the pup has grown a few months and can get some traction and force, not so much. Then you have the added issue of your dog's reactivity. As a responsible citizen you want to keep your dog under control, so suddenly you start to wind the lead six times round your hand - a dangerous practice in itself - and pull him in tight. This really is not going to work!

Here's an exercise for you to change this entirely. Start this indoors, in a place where your dog feels calm and comfortable. If her anxiety is such that the sight of the lead worries her as she fears she has to go on a walk, work in a room without the "walk" association - the living room, perhaps, or your garden. Whatever gear you usually walk your dog in, work on a soft collar and lead for now. Lots more about kit coming up in Book 2.

Key Lead Skill no.1: Keeping the lead loose

1. Have your dog on a longish lead (6-8 feet, at least 2 metres)
2. Stand still and let the dog pull to the end of the lead, wherever she wants to go
3. Keep your hand close to your hip. Tuck your thumb into your belt if necessary
4. Wait. Wait till the lead slackens the tiniest bit. It doesn't matter why - don't judge. You may think you'll need to wait forever, but it's usually only 20 seconds or so at most
5. As soon as you feel the lead relax - *for any reason at all, even by accident* - call your dog and reward her with a tasty treat at your knee
6. Repeat Steps 2-5 till she understands that it's up to her to keep the lead loose

This exercise is simplicity itself. It tells your dog that you are no longer the one that's pulling. Your hands are soft. It's her choice if she pulls. Given a little time, she'll choose not to pull at all.

If your dog is in the habit of lurching to the end of the lead as soon as it's on, you may have to repeat this exercise frequently. In most cases we need repeat it only long enough to get the new system of lead-holding into our own heads. Once *we've* got it, our dog will get it.

Dogs are doers, not not-doers. So your dog is learning to keep the lead loose, rather than not to pull on it. See the difference?

What you accept is what you get

ACTION STEP 11:

Every time you put the lead on your dog, you need to remember to keep your hand close to you and wait for her to slacken the lead. If you are in the habit of putting on the lead and letting your dog pull you to the door, then that is what will happen.

What you reward is what you get.

And there are few better rewards for many dogs then heading out through that door! Even your super-anxious dog may pull to the door, as she's on full alert for what she may find the other side - her hormones are racing. Your dog needs to learn that - no matter what happened in the past - things have now changed, which means pulling on the lead will get her nowhere. Dogs aren't dumb. They do what works.

From now on you will never move until the lead is slack.

NEVER!

If you find your arm floating out, recapture it and tuck it into your belt! If it keeps happening, put your partner or one of your children on "arm-watch." They'll love having the chance of pointing out your mistake to you!

In this chapter we have learnt:

- To take a fresh look at things we take for granted
- That building your dog's confidence and connection with you is key
- You can relax
- Your dog can relax
- Anxiety has just been dialled back several notches!

Chapter 10 Dog Body Language

"I'm no threat!"

Unlike us, dogs don't rate vocalisation very highly. Yes - I know that some of us with reactive dogs hear too much of their opinions! But when dogs vocalise it tends to be about their emotional state - fear, excitement, alarm, pain, and so on. When they want to "speak" to each other, they use their highly sophisticated and silent body language.

And if we want a chance of joining in this conversation, we need to learn this powerful lingo! There are some terrific visual resources that help you to understand what your dog is saying, and you'll find some good ones in the Resources Section.

Body signals can be large or tiny. For instance a slow blink of the eyes is a calming signal. Staring is rude - not just in dogs! - and while a dog may need to look at another dog to study whether that dog is a threat or not, they should not do it in a threatening way.

Imagine this: you're sitting on a bus, and the man opposite you has an enormous nose. You feel the need to study this extraordinary nose, so you choose a moment when he's looking away to have a peer at it. Then he looks back towards you. You quickly focus on the shop you can see past his shoulder, or your watch - anything to demonstrate that you weren't staring at him!

Dogs will do the same thing - they'll slow-blink their eyes to break their stare, they'll start sniffing the ground, they'll turn and look somewhere else, or they'll turn their whole body away. The last two are called a "lookaway" and once you start noticing your dog doing lookaways you'll know that there is something she's avoiding looking at. This could be a strange dog, a strange dog staring at her, a person, whatever creature or thing worries her.

At the same time as looking away, or sniffing the ground, your dog can keep the worrying thing in her peripheral vision. Dogs have 270° vision, as against our measly 180° range. So they can turn their head right away - lessening any sign of conflict - while still remaining able to study the other dog or person. This is clearly an essential survival skill.

Two lookaways

There are other signs you'll be looking out for, such as lip-licking, yawning, shaking-off, which all indicate anxiety. The shaking-off is settling the coat down again after the hairs have all stood on end - just like us when we get a fright, have goose bumps, then do a quick shiver to snap out of it. It's a sign that the dog *was* alarmed and anxious, but has decided to move on.

A quick dart of the tongue as a lip-lick, when it's not to do with food, is a calming signal. It tells the other dog that he's a little bit worried. Yawning is also more associated with release of tension - a sign that the dog *was* tense.

Tail-wagging is much misunderstood. There is a whole language of the tail! Dogs will even wag their tail to one side when they greet someone they know. And of course there are variables depending on the type of dog and type of tail (some dogs, like terriers, carry their tails very straight and erect a lot of the time). Many is the person who has been bitten by a dog whose tail was wagging! A wagging tail is simply evidence of agitation in the dog.

The elevation of the tail and the speed of wagging have a lot to do with it. Think soppy Golden Retriever with sinuous body movement, soft eyes, mouth slack and open, tongue lolling, and mid-height gently waving tail, as the epitome of the friendly dog. Think fierce Doberman with tall, stiff, erect body, stiff tail, leaning forward, straight legs, mouth shut, staring eyes, frown, frozen position - move calmly away from this dog without looking at him.

Yes - before my inbox explodes with protests - there are lovely, friendly Dobermans, and there are Golden Retrievers who bite. I'm giving you an example of what the typical body language is saying in a breed you should recognise. Dobermans have been bred to look fierce as they are wanted as guard dogs, so breeders have selected for these traits.

Grinning with eyes closed: some dogs will do this to show that they mean no harm. It's what you see in those dreadful internet videos about "guilty" dogs. More often than not, the dog has no idea why their owner is cross with them, and they're saying "Please don't punish me". It's pretty pathetic that people set this up, video it, then put the video online to laugh at the unfortunate dog.

You may notice the tense lines around the mouth and cheeks - especially if you have a smooth-coated dog. His ears may be doing a dance, and running through several signals in succession. Some dogs will move into slow motion, maybe creeping on their belly. Some will dangle a front paw puppy-style to show they're no threat. Not every dog does every single signal, but they will run through a sequence of them, from a little bit anxious right up to "Get me outa here!", which is one step away from a bite.

Bites

Dogs never "bite out of the blue". There's always been a procession of signs that show the dog's increasing discomfort. Trouble is, unsocialised dogs and humans tend not to be able to read them. This is the reason for all those heart-stoppingly gruesome internet videos of babies crawling over dogs and pulling their ears. Some of those babies are a whisker away from getting bitten. Some do get bitten - then guess whose fault it is? And the doting parents see none of the dog's discomfort and allow all sorts of intrusions into the dog's dignity. The poor dog is trapped! He's saying,

- Look away = Please don't come near me
- Moving away = I wish I could get away from you
- Blink = I'm not a threat to you
- Lip-lick = This is worrying - where's my escape route?
- Stiff body = This should show them I'm not in the mood
- Staring with whites of eyes showing = I'm really *really* not happy about this
- Wrinkling lip = Would you just leave me alone?
- Growl = I'm serious - leave me alone! (see Chapter 6)
- Snap = Look! I have teeth! I will use them if I have to!
- Bite = I told you 9 times to clear off. Why didn't you get the message?

Breed variations

Not all dogs are the same shape, size, or coat-type. And clearly these things can make a difference. A short-coated dog's signs are in general much easier to read.

If your dog is arousing a lot of suspicion in other dogs, there may be something you can do to help. If he has a mop of hair over his eyes, trim it! Be sure he can see clearly. If you were in a frightening situation, you wouldn't want to be trying to look through a thick veil! My Border Collie, Rollo, when young, had what I thought a very fetching curled-up coat over his shoulders. The hair swept up and forward instead of lying back flat. This could be misconstrued by another dog as raised hackles - a sign of fear or aggression in a dog, who is standing his hair up to make himself look as big as possible. So we took to smoothing his coat down before meeting other dogs.

An unwarranted intrusion

I watched a scene once where a street-dog was happily moving amongst the crowds at a fair, snuffling the ground for food and minding his own business. A woman spotted him, put on a daft smile, and silently reached down and scratched his bum. The dog spun round with a bark, before moving off and looking for food elsewhere. "That dog nearly bit me!" the woman complained loudly to whoever would listen. Dogs are so quick: if he'd wanted to bite her she would have been bitten! This dog was simply telling her to clear off.

And in my view the dog was quite justified. How would she have felt if a stranger had put on a silly expression, then scratched *her* bum? I bet she'd have had something to say!

Dogs are not our playthings. They are sentient beings with their own opinions and feelings. We expect them to fit into our lives, for our benefit. The least we can do is have some understanding of what they are thinking, feeling - and saying.

Honour your dog!

As you espouse choice-based training, you are going to find that your dog can manage situations rather better than you thought - if you let her get on with it! Of course, you need to keep everyone safe, and if your dog has bitten then your first priority is to ensure it can't happen again - more about that in the next book.

But for now, you want to encourage her to express her body language freely. This means your lead must be loose so that she *can!* She can't look calm and relaxed when her head is being held up and she can't breathe properly. When you see a dog or person or whatever alarms her, you can relax your hands on your loose lead and watch what your dog does. She may stare at them for a bit, then turn her head back to you and say "Can we go now?" Perfect! Off you both go, without anyone having got upset. If she starts to get taller and stiffer, creeps forward, shuts her mouth - or any of the other signs you will now recognise, then that's when you decide to go, and take her happily with you.

ACTION STEP 12:

Research Dog Body Language thoroughly and start spotting what your dog is saying and when. Check out the Resources Section for where to look. Notice the signals he uses and those he doesn't - and when you see them in another dog. Start to notice your reactive dog's signals earlier and earlier so that you can catch the moment he seems unhappy about another dog or person or rattly plastic bag and relieve the tension by removing him from the scene.

In this chapter we have:

- Had an immersion course in a foreign language
- Learned to respect our dog's opinions
- Remembered that it's all about choice - give your dog a choice, and applaud a good choice

Chapter 11 Health aspects

Neutering

This chapter is all about the physical side of your dog. I'll start off with the thorny subject of neutering. Remember, I'm not a vet, so we are only interested here in the effects neutering may or may not have on our dog's reactivity and state of mind. And these effects can be major! So I'm not looking at neutering as a population control strategy, neutering which is essential for some medical reason, or neutering as a convenience option for the owner. Nor am I looking at the evidence which shows increased medical and orthopaedic issues associated with neutering - especially early neutering (anything before age 1, roughly speaking).

And if your dog is already neutered, don't skip this section! It may explain a few things for you, and you need to know for your next dog.

Myth: neutering will calm my dog down

Neutering will remove certain body parts from your dog which will stop the flow of the associated hormones through the body. Your dog will no longer be able to reproduce, and will not be driven by sexual urges *as much*. A neutered male may still mount and tie with a bitch on heat - he's just firing blanks. Neutered dogs as well as entire dogs and bitches can still get sexually excited by the presence of a bitch in season, which is why bitches on heat are not allowed at competitions which require focus from the competitors, such as Obedience, Dancing with Dogs, and so on. Most dog training classes will not take a bitch in season - even if all the other dogs in the class are female or neutered. Too exciting!

If your dog is an escapologist and a rambler at the moment, and you think that that is a sexually-driven activity, neutering will only take the edge off his enthusiasm. If you want his habits to change you need to apply some training to the problem. In other words, neutering is not a quick fix, though it may well be a good step in this case.

Nor will it "calm down" your young dog, who is behaving as … a young dog. Possibly just a young dog in need of training. In fact, studies have shown that the opposite is true! Your neutered dog or bitch is apparently likely to be *more* excitable than an intact dog.

Myth: neutering will make my dog less aggressive

And this is the big one, and our focus in these books. It has been shown, in a number of recent scientific studies, that neutering - especially early neutering - *will increase sound sensitivity, touch sensitivity, fears, and aggression*, in both males and females. In some cases that increase is "significant" or "highly significant". People-directed aggression in females, for instance, was significantly elevated in the neutered bitches studied. (See the Resources Section for chapter and verse on this.) That's what those studies found. A lot more research is needed to get more answers, and these studies can take years to produce reliable results.

These unfortunate outcomes are - of course - not guaranteed to happen if you neuter your dog! But it's important to be aware that they just may happen. And if they complicate an already complicated situation, that's not helpful.

Neutering has the potential to make your dog worse.

Isn't this a social obligation?

There are cultural differences across the globe. In some cultures neutering is referred to as "getting the dog fixed" - as if the dog has arrived in some way faulty and needs repair. In fact in such cultures it's rare to find unneutered dogs except those earmarked for breeding or those belonging to people who couldn't care less.

On the other hand, there are plenty of cultures where it's normal to leave dogs entire, even mixed-sex dogs in the same household. In some European countries it is considered barbaric to mutilate dogs, and neutering of either sex is usually only done for medical reasons. At the other extreme we have cultures where people are vociferous in declaring that all dogs should be neutered and it is our duty as a citizen to do this.

Those who decide to neuter as a means of population control are often the ones who would not leave their dog straying anyway. Those who don't care, don't care. So it's pretty inefficient at preventing unwanted puppies - just look at the bulging shelters. If you are able to manage a household of unneutered dogs without mishap (as many breeders do), then you will have more freedom in your choice. Naturally, any litters resulting from your intact dogs should be carefully planned. Finding the right homes for puppies can be a daunting task. Being able to adopt this strategy may depend on your individual dog - some can be very determined to find a mate!

So I'm simply suggesting that you need to change your mindset from neutering being an automatic next step for your puppy to seeing that you have a choice in this.

The one unarguable fact of neutering is that it is irreversible. So any changes made cannot be unmade. If neutering your reactive dog causes his or her reactivity to double in frequency and intensity, you are now up the creek without a paddle. There is no way back.

A halfway house could be veterinary intervention in the form of "chemical castration" or drugs which control the extreme symptoms some bitches experience, such as false pregnancies, extended and irregular seasons. Such interventions are temporary and may be worth looking into with your vet to see how behaviour is affected.

Young and cautious or fearful males *can* become very aggressive in appearance when their source of testosterone dries up overnight.

Females *can* become unpredictable after neutering - especially if there were complications seen earlier, like becoming very spooky or reactive before a season, or having difficult false pregnancies.

Whatever you decide to do with your dog's sexual status, please look into the literature carefully first. Do not listen to the old wives' tales about neutering "calming the dog down". *This step is irreversible!* If you find things have got worse after neutering, there is now no way back.

In case you think I am on a mission to ban neutering, I can tell you that only one of my four dogs is entire at the time of writing. You have to decide what is right for your situation. I just want you to realise that there's more to this than meets the eye, and *you do have a choice.*

If you have already neutered your dog, don't waste energy on recriminations or what-ifs. It's water under the bridge. As ever, we'll work with what we have right now.

(IN)ACTION STEP 13:

If your dog is still entire, study the literature before taking this step. As you are reading this book and have presumably already got a problem of fear or aggression, *don't neuter right now.* You have plenty of time later to do this, if it's the right decision for your dog. *Purely from a behavioural point of view,* do not neuter a reactive bitch before her second season, and do not neuter a reactive dog till he is mature (2-3 years old, depending on breed). Wait till you have worked through this program then see how he or she is. Remember you need to discuss all this with a vet!

Medications

There are a number of meds that may help your dog, many developed from those used for psychological problems in humans. If your dog's fears and reactivity are so severe that he cannot lead a normal life, then a visit to a veterinary behaviourist is indicated. Apart from fear of strangers and/or strange dogs, these fears may include OCD (Obsessive Compulsive Disorders) like stalking and chasing lights, shadows, or reflections; extreme Separation Anxiety which causes physical damage to the dog; extreme fear of storms or traffic, for instance, which cause panic and danger.

There are a few questions you need to ask your vet before you embark on a course of prescribed medication for your dog:

1. How long will it be before it takes effect? This can be weeks or months.
2. Can I stop the medication abruptly or must the dog be weaned off it?
3. What known side-effects are there?

Many prescription medications have side-effects. Steroids, for instance - often prescribed for skin problems - are known to cause an increase in aggression in some dogs. See if there is an alternative you can use.

While you're at the vet, check out thyroid imbalance and pain. Who doesn't feel aggressive when suffering from earache or toothache? Not to mention a twinge in your back or hips that gets you every time someone touches you! Some touch sensitivity can be an early symptom of serious illness.

Some people think that using medication for their dog is in some way an admission of failure on their part. If the dog is helped by medication, then go for it! Would you deny this help to your child? It's not a moral issue - it just is as it is.

Over-the-counter medications

There is a whole slew of OTC remedies available, from herbal mixtures to flower remedies. Check with your vet that they can do no harm, then give them a go. For some dogs they work brilliantly, for others not at all.

There are quick-acting remedies, often marketed for fear of fireworks. And I have found Bach flower remedies work fast (if they're going to work at all).

ACTION STEP 14:

If you haven't yet booked that vet check suggested in Chapter 4, get onto it now!

Other therapies

There are many canine therapists now available to help your dog, for example:

- TTouch (previously known as Tellington Touch)
- Canine Massage
- Bowen Technique

These all use touching techniques which ease your dog's body (and therefore mind), uncover any hidden or intermittent pain points, and can improve body balance (and therefore mental balance too).

TTouch is known for its superb calming abilities. I have seen frantic and anxious dogs reduced to a sighing furry stretched-out heap on the floor after a skilled practitioner has spent a few minutes "hitting the spot".

It's well worth seeking out a local accredited practitioner and see how it goes for your dog. This is not New Age woolliness - they have governing bodies and exams: see the Resources Section. Some people find the therapies so effective for their precious dog (or cat or parrot or you-name-it) that they go on to study and qualify as a practitioner themselves.

In this chapter we have learnt that:

- Neutering may make your reactive, fearful dog worse
- This step cannot be undone
- Medication may help
- Canine touch therapies are very likely to help - and be very popular with your dog!

Conclusion

So now you know!

- You have a far greater understanding of what's going on and why
- You are no longer blaming your dog
- You are no longer blaming your dog's history
- You are no longer blaming yourself!
- and, understandable as it may be, you know it's pointless blaming those who misled you in the past

Furthermore, you are now on the road to some solid changes which will make a world of difference to the both of you. You can see your dog with new eyes, you can show empathy with her, and you can face the future together.

One student said to me when arriving for her second session, that if they had been at the stage they now were with their dog, they wouldn't have needed to call me out. In other words, just working on the information in this first book made a massive difference to the way they understood their dog and why he was doing what he was doing.

With understanding comes love and patience. Patience, love, and encouragement will be needed in spades in the next two books! You can make dramatic changes in your dog's worldview - but it isn't an overnight fix. You'll be taking a couple of steps forward, then one back, a lot of the time. Provided you keep your eyes on your end goal, you'll get there.

And what is your end goal? It should be simple - and perhaps not what you thought when you embarked on this program! Your dog does not have to be everyone's friend. She may enjoy the company of some dog-friends she knows well, or she may say - like my Lacy aka Greta Garbo - "I want to be alone". (Garbo actually said she wanted to be "let alone", which is even more to the point.) Some of us love parties and some of us hate them - allow your dog to choose what camp she is comfortable in, and honour her decision.

A practical and sensible goal would be for your dog to feel happier and more confident when out, for you to have techniques and tricks up your sleeve to cope with any eventuality, and for you both to enjoy your walks - both on-lead on the street, and off-lead in the safety of forest and wide open spaces.

Head to Book 2: **Change for your Growly Dog!** *Action steps to build confidence in your fearful, aggressive, or reactive dog* and let's get to it!

Resources

For a very thorough, in-depth, approach, where I will be on hand to answer all your questions, go to

brilliantfamilydog.teachable.com

where you'll find info about the online course which takes all this to the next level, giving you personal support and encouragement as well as all the lessons and techniques you need to change your life with your Growly Dog.

For a free taster course: **www.brilliantfamilydog.com/growly**

And for loads of articles on Growly Dogs and Choice Training, go to **www.brilliantfamilydog.com** where you'll also find a course on solving everyday dog and puppy problems.

You'll also find the **Essential Skills for a Brilliant Family Dog** series of e-books helpful. Take a holistic view of your relationship with your dog and work on new skills inside the house as well as when you're out. If your dog has always had to be kept on lead because you were afraid he was not safe, you'll definitely need Book 4 for your new life!

Book 1 Calm Down! *Step-by-Step to a Calm, Relaxed, and Brilliant Family Dog*
Book 2 Leave it! *How to teach Amazing Impulse Control to your Brilliant Family Dog*
Book 3 Let's Go! *Enjoy Companionable Walks with your Brilliant Family Dog*

Book 4 Here Boy! *Step-by-step to a Stunning Recall from your Brilliant Family Dog*

And you'll be pleased to know that Book 1 is currently free at all e-book stores!

Here are the links to all the resources mentioned in this book:

Books by other authors:

I'll Be Home Soon: How to Prevent and Treat Separation Anxiety by Patricia McConnell, pub First Stone, 2010

Control Unleashed: Creating a Focused and Confident Dog by Leslie McDevitt, pub Clean Run Productions LLC, 2007
http://controlunleashed.net/book.html

Behavior Adjustment Training 2.0: New Practical Techniques for Fear, Frustration, and Aggression in Dogs by Grisha Stewart, pub Dogwise Publishing, 2016

Websites:
www.muzzleupproject.com - all things muzzle
www.goodfordogs.co.uk/products - Wiggles Wags and Whiskers Freedom Harness - UK and Europe [This is me. If you buy from me I will benefit financially, but it won't cost you any more.]
http://2houndswholesale.com/Where-to-Buy.html - Wiggles Wags and Whiskers Freedom Harness - rest of the world
https://www.youtube.com/watch?v=1OHEB41yRdU - one of many calming sound recordings
https://positively.com/dog-wellness/dog-enrichment/music-for-dogs/canine-noise-phobia-series/ - for desensitisation
http://en.turid-rugaas.no/calming-signals---the-art-of-survival.html - dog body language

http://www.youtube.com/watch?v=00_9JPltXHI - dog body language
http://www.youtube.com/watch?v=bstvG_SUzMo - dog body language
http://www.doggiedrawings.net/#!freeposters/ckm8 - Lili Chin's fantastic dog body language illustrations. Please respect her requests re sharing her copyright material - she is very generous
http://www.kendalshepherd.com/the-canine-commandments/ - The Canine Ladder of Aggression
www.hemopet.org - Dr Jean Dodds, authority on Hypothyroidism and dog allergies
www.allaboutdogfood.co.uk Independent UK reference for what's really in that bag
www.rawmeatybones.com A vet shows you how to get started on a raw diet

Force-free training hubs:
http://www.apdt.co.uk/dog-owners/local-dog-trainers - UK resource for force-free trainers
http://www.petprofessionalguild.com/PetGuildMembers - global resource for force-free trainers
http://grishastewart.com/cbati-directory/ - global resource for specialist Certified BAT Instructors

Neutering resources quoted:
http://www.thelabradorsite.com/should-i-have-my-labrador-neutered-the-latest-evidence/ - The effects of neutering on health and behaviour: a summary Accessed 2016

http://www.atftc.com/health/SNBehaviorBoneDataSnapShot.pdf
Behavioral and Physical Effects of Spaying and Neutering Domestic Dogs (Canis familiaris)
Summary of findings detailed in a Masters thesis submitted to and accepted by Hunter College
by Parvene Farhoody in May, 2010
Accessed 2016

http://www.caninesports.com/uploads/1/5/3/1/15319800/vizsla_javma_study.pdf
AVMA, Vol 244, No. 3, February 1, 2014
Evaluation of the risk and age of onset of cancer and behavioral disorders in gonadectomized Vizslas
M. Christine Zink DVM PhD, Parvene Farhoody MA, Samra E. Elser BS, Lynda D. Ruffini, Tom A. Gibbons MS, Randall H. Rieger PhD
Accessed 2016

http://saova.org/articles/Early%20SN%20and%20Behavior.pdf
Non-reproductive Effects of Spaying and Neutering on Behavior in Dogs
Deborah L. Duffy PhD, and James A. Serpell PhD
Center for the Interaction of Animals and Society, School of Veterinary Medicine, University of Pennsylvania
Accessed 2016

Alternative practitioner societies:
www.ttouch.com
www.ttouchtteam.co.uk
www.k9-massageguild.co.uk
www.massageawareness.com
www.caninebowentechnique.com

Essential Skills for your *Growly* but
Brilliant Family Dog

Book 2

Change for your Growly Dog!

Action steps to build confidence
in your fearful, aggressive, or reactive dog

Beverley Courtney

Introduction

You know your dog has a lovely personality. She's smashing at home - loves playing with the children, does what you ask, settles quietly when you're busy. But outside … or perhaps when visitors come … you have a different dog. The ruckus she makes when confronted with a strange person, a strange dog, even a strange *bag*, is upsetting for you and frightening for everyone else. She ducks and dives, lunges and surges, barks, snarls, and growls: who wouldn't be alarmed?

We've looked at

- what is happening,
- why it's happening,
- why it's getting worse,
- and what you can start changing to begin the transformation you're looking for.

That's all in Book 1 of this series.

We're now going to go into far greater detail to give you strategies and techniques to avoid trouble (and if necessary to get you out of it!). These strategies will enable you to change *your* mindset, and then change your dog's mindset. If she's to change, then you have to change too!

But nowhere am I going to tell you it's your fault, or your dog's fault, or the fault of your dog's previous owners, or the fault of the alignment of the stars at your dog's birth. Blaming is totally unproductive. You need to start where you are, with what you've got, and move forward from there.

So we will advance in a cheerily positive state of mind! You'll come to see that what I give you are the missing parts of the puzzle, and you'll be able to see why harsher methods recommended to you in the past have not worked.

And why me?

Spending a lot of time, in my training school Good for Dogs, with "the dog owner in the street" - the family pet owner - has shown me how people learn best, what they need to know, and what they actually *don't* need to know. Being blinded by science is not going to make the training more accessible!

Some of these dog-owners were facing problems with their "growly" dog. Some had tried other avenues and not liked what they were told to do to their dog, whom they loved. Others had seen the tv programs and heard the "advice" from fellow dog owners and knew that way wasn't for them, so they sought out a force-free trainer.

Each new person and each new dog offers a new challenge. I've learned to be adaptable and customise my training for the individual in front of me. What I can say is that this system has a phenomenal success rate. Once the owner is prepared to make some changes and put in the necessary flying hours, they invariably get the transformation they wanted. They may need to adjust their end-goals a little, but that's easy to do once they understand their dog better. Perhaps their dog will never be the life and soul of the party - and that's fine. Just don't force him to go to parties!

See how things started working quickly for Fitz:

> "The past few walks I've seen a huge difference in his behavior in general. He notices the other dogs but doesn't make an effort to lunge or struggle, he makes noise but it is not as dramatic. It's a small step in his social issues, but a big relief that he is learning."

So where do I start?

This book, Book 2 **Change for your Growly Dog!** *Action steps to build confidence in your fearful, aggressive, or reactive dog,* stands alone, but you'll get much more out of it if you've first read the first book in this series, **Why is my Dog so Growly?** *Teach your fearful, aggressive, or reactive dog confidence through understanding.* All the gaps in your knowledge - the whys, whats, and wherefores - will be nagging at the back of your mind and will continually interfere with your understanding of the material in this book. So I recommend you go and get Book 1 and read that first. And to make this easier, there's a special offer for Book 1! (Who can resist a special offer?) Complete clarity is my aim.

So these three books are best consumed together, in order.

- The first tells you what's going on and why - and some of this may surprise you. It's essential to understand a problem before attempting to fix it. This section should bring you lots of "Aha!" moments.

- The second book goes into the detail of what you're going to change and how, what approaches will work best, and what you need to make it all work. Lots of Lessons in this section. And much of this will involve change for *you:* exciting!

- And the third gets you out there with your dog, enjoying a new way of walking and interacting with her, and making the scene at the start of this Introduction - mercifully! - a thing of the past. Lots more Lessons here, and Troubleshooting sections to cover all the "what ifs" you'll come up with.

My suggestion is to read through the book first, then while your brain is filtering and processing this information, you can go back to the start and work through the Action Steps and Lessons with your dog.

For ease of reading, your dog is going to be a he or a she as the whim takes me. He and she will learn the exact same way and have similar responses.

There will be just a few occasions when we're discussing only a male or a female, and that will be clear.

So let's get stuck into Chapter 1!

Section 1

Training basics

Chapter 1

Before we embark on the Lessons, there's an important area we need to cover. Read this now and you'll have plenty of time to be sure you and your dog are properly suited and booted before you get started.

Equipment that will help you ... and equipment to avoid like the plague

I'm going to show you not only what equipment you need, but also what equipment you *don't need*, and - importantly! - what equipment to avoid at all costs.

First of all, let's take a quick diversion into anatomy. There is a myth that a dog's neck is somehow different from ours and can withstand the crushing effect of a collar cutting into the throat without any damage whatsoever. This is clearly nonsense. You only have to hear a dog choking as he heaves into his collar or see his eyeballs sticking out, his tongue going blue, and his face creased with the strain to know how wrong this myth is.

In fact, physiologically a dog's neck is *virtually identical to ours*. The trachea, thyroid gland, and oesophagus are all in much the same place. The nerves and blood supply to the brain are similar.

Now, imagine a constricting force on your own neck. What's going to be affected? Your eyes, your throat, your thyroid. lack of blood to the head, distress, fear, pain, and a feeling of being trapped and threatened. Some of these things are temporary, but some can have a permanent effect, and while the damage can be physical, mental damage will also be caused by this pain and aggravation, resulting in stress and anxiety.

Every time this happens, your dog is making a firm association that "walking on a lead means pain and bad things," which can quickly translate to "being outside is dangerous".

So if it's so bad, why on earth do dogs do it?

Dogs, as you'll oft hear me say, are simple creatures. They are doers, and they do what works. They aren't straining to pull you somewhere because they have a secret agenda or want to show you who's boss. They are pulling into their collar because they want to get somewhere and you usually follow them!

When they're very young, they don't have to pull that hard for the indulgent owner to stretch out an arm and follow. How often do you think they have to try this before it's a habit? Once? Twice? How often does a child need to see where the cake is kept to know which kitchen cupboard to head for? Once, I'd say!

When the dog gets a bit older, larger, and stronger, his owner becomes less forgiving, and he has to pull a lot harder. Sooner or later the pulling wears down the owner's resolve, and they follow their dog. Their dog is experiencing considerable pain and anxiety, but owner and dog are now in a vicious circle of pulling and counter-pulling. This is why the lead responsiveness and parking exercises you'll find in the Key Lead Skills are so important to work on. You don't need to pull the lead or yank it. Just don't follow!

It's going to be very hard for your anxious dog to remain calm with a collar digging into her neck - more on why later on.

But my dog is big and strong!

Your dog doesn't need to be large to damage your shoulders with her pulling. A small and determined terrier can exert a lot of force on the lead. If you have a dog who already pulls like a train as soon as the lead is clipped on, then you'll need to dress her in something different while you train her to walk nicely on her collar.

Collars are very useful for attaching ID tags and for quickly holding onto in the heat of the moment, but they aren't essential dog gear. Your dog can wear a harness whenever you're out - provided it's the right kind - or, of course, your dog can wear both.

Collars

Cricket is comfortable in her velvet martingale collar

Some dogs don't like their collar being touched. They've been hauled about on the collar or dragged somewhere they didn't want to go. I'm horrified when I see people literally dragging a fearful and reluctant puppy along behind them on his bum!

Keep this in mind if you have a rescue dog: rescue dogs may have had a boatload of unpleasant experiences and can be very hand-shy. You might see this as they duck and dive when a hand reaches out toward them. They may also try to grab the hand with their mouth or just freeze in position. Remember not to wallow in "Ahh, someone's hit him!" We start from where we are.

You need to begin by changing your dog's view of a collar-hold to a thing of beauty, not fear. Here's an exercise you can do repeatedly, perhaps when you're relaxing after dinner. Keep it brief and fun.

Lesson 2 The Collar Hold revisited (from Book 1)

1. Have a supply of scrummy treats to hand
2. Have one treat ready in one hand, and with the other hand reach out and touch the side of your dog's face - just for a second - then remove your hand, feed the treat
3. Repeat Step 2 until she's happy to let you touch her face
4. Repeat Step 2, but reach and touch the side of her neck - just for a second - then remove your hand, feed the treat
5. Repeat Step 4 till she's happy
6. Repeat Step 4, but touch the collar for a second before feeding the treat
7. Keep going till you can slip a finger into her collar, remove your hand - feed treat
8. Eventually you'll be able to slide your hand softly into her collar, with the back of your hand resting against her neck, and walk a few steps with her beside you before feeding the treat
9. When you reach towards your dog's collar she'll stay still and allow you to hold it then stay with you

Watchpoints:

- This will take as long as it takes. Maybe one session of a couple of minutes, maybe ten sessions - doesn't matter
- Be sure to remove your touching hand before feeding the treat
- Work *very fast* - touch-remove-treat, touch-remove-treat, keep it light and fun
- You are never pulling on this collar, not even gripping it firmly
- The goal is to be able to slip your hand into your dog's collar whenever you need to

In time your dog should see your hand approaching and offer her collar to you, then stay still while you slip your hand in, with the back of your hand resting against her neck. This contact will become very comforting to your reactive dog.

Choose:

The collar should be comfortable to wear, easy to put on and take off, and quick-drying if your dog enjoys swimming. It can be soft webbing, soft leather, or woven fabric - this last is especially useful for fast-growing small puppies as you slot the fabric onto the buckle wherever you want.

For older pups and dogs I prefer snap collars to buckle collars because you can adjust the size millimetre by millimetre instead of being stuck with pre-punched holes. Buckle collars can come undone.

Martingale collars made of soft webbing are particularly useful for sighthounds, bull breeds, and any other dog whose neck is larger than its head. These slip over the head and can fit very loosely on the dog's neck - but once the lead is attached they are impossible to back out of. Adjust this collar carefully, fitting it so it doesn't tighten and constrict the neck. It's not meant to be a choke collar, just not slip off.

Any piece of equipment is only as strong as its weakest part - so check clips, fabric, stitching, the soldering on rings, and so on, before you buy. Don't go cheap.

Avoid:

Avoid collars that work by hurting. This includes prong collars, slip collars, chain collars, half-chain collars, choke collars, and *anything* that uses a battery. (An exception to the no-battery rule is the "buzz" collar for deaf dogs, which vibrates like your mobile phone and serves to catch their attention.)

If you have any of these in your armoury, please destroy them - don't pass them on to be used on some other hapless dog. You may have been told that you had to use these barbaric devices in order to gain control over your dog.

Here's news for you: *your dog is going to learn to control herself!* You don't walk with your child handcuffed to your arm - you hold his hand gently and teach him what you want him to learn.

Remember your dog's neck is just as delicate and sensitive as your own neck. Or your child's neck. Thankfully more and more countries are making these instruments of torture illegal.

Harness

Oakley on a loose lead in his comfy harness

Choose:

The harness I personally favour is the *Wiggles Wags and Whiskers Freedom Harness*, listed in the Resources section at the end of this book along with a link to a demo video. You are not so much looking for something to prevent pulling, rather you want a harness designed to promote balance. You are looking for a harness which attaches to a double connection lead in two places - in front and on the back. You want a harness that does not impede shoulder movement, does not chafe or rub, and has the effect of balancing your dog.

The object of using a harness is to prevent the dog pulling into a collar and damaging herself. It can also make Loose Lead Walking a doddle, as the dog has to support herself on her own four feet - without using you as a fifth leg - but it has to be the right sort of harness! Look for one which has the same effect as the one shown in the video.

"But I want my dog to stop barking - I don't want to learn loose lead walking!" Yes, you do. Walking calmly without discomfort and a fight at every step will help you enormously when we come to changing your dog's mindset when she enters the fray of Outside. For a complete step-by-step course, see *Let's Go: Enjoy Companionable Walks with your Brilliant Family Dog*, Book 3 in the series of **Essential Skills for a Brilliant Family Dog** (more info in the Resources section).

Avoid:

Some harnesses are designed to encourage the animal to pull, like a horse in harness pulling a cart or a husky pulling a sled. They aren't unpleasant: they're just not the right tool for this job. Others are sold to prevent pulling. Sadly many of these work by hurting the dog - by cutting under the armpits or by tightening and staying tight. Your dog will soon be pulling through the pain just as she did with her collar.

Head Halters

Coco at 9 weeks happy in his head halter

These require some skill to use humanely, but are useful if your dog continually has her nose on the ground, or has a habit of leaping out at passers-by to grab them. If the dog lurches to the end of the lead and is stopped abruptly, the head collar could cause her head to twist. It's essential that the lead stays loose when she's wearing it, and you don't flick or jerk it. Gentle pressure to turn the head is what you need and this takes a bit of practice. The best way is to slide your hand right down to where the lead clips onto the head collar and move the dog's head from there. This will ensure you don't yank the lead. Sometimes head collars are promoted to keep control of your dog's head so she can't bite anyone.

Many dogs dislike the head halter, largely because it's just been whammed on their face and tweaked. So acclimatise your dog gradually to this new gear, always associating the sight or touch of the head halter with good things - it could take weeks till she's keen to wear it.

As I said above, your dog is going to learn to control herself (exciting!) and I don't recommend these for trying to change a reactive dog.

Choose:

Only use a "fixed" head halter (example, *Gentle Leader*). Some figure-of-eight head collars will slacken as soon as the pulling stops and are safe to use.

Avoid:

A slip halter, or slip collar-halter combination - all of which tighten and stay tight if the dog pulls.

Leads

Leads are much more meaningful than you may think!

Perhaps you see your lead as a controlling device, a way to move or restrain your dog. What we are working on here is to give the control to the dog, so she can exercise *self-control*. We want her to have the choice to keep the lead loose. Revolutionary, I know! So think of the lead as a connection between you and your dog - as well as insurance that she won't end up under a bus. You may be surprised to learn that a loose lead will actually *lessen* the chance of your dog lunging out! Really … more about this later on.

In order to give your dog the freedom to walk easily beside you, the lead must be long enough. Six feet is a good length. If the lead is too short, as soon as she moves an inch she's on a tight lead! Most leads you find in pet shops are ridiculously short - three feet or so.

When you're holding the lead, break that habit of winding it five times around your hand then continually flicking and jerking it! Many people have no idea that they're doing this, but every flick or jab is another nail in the coffin of your relationship with your dog.

The lead should be held loosely in your sensitive hand. If you need to prevent yourself jabbing the lead, tuck your thumb into your belt or pocket to keep your hand still.

If you have to keep your dog on-lead all the time, you'll also do well with a 15-foot long line for when you're in an open space or field. (Don't use this line when you're on the road!) In fact, you'll need this for some of the training we'll be doing. This length is comfortable to handle and gives your dog the freedom to mooch about and snuffle without danger of her running off. It's important to "flake the line" in your hand - to have it in loose bows or figures-of-eight instead of coils that can tighten and trap a finger. It's the same system sailors use for the rope attached to a fishing net - so that it can pay out freely without getting caught, or catch a leg in a loop and take a sailor overboard with it.

More about all this in the Key Lead Skills in a little while.

Choose:

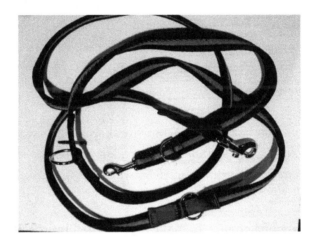

You want a soft fabric or leather lead, at least six feet in length. Some people like a light rope or plaited lead. Remember this is for a dog, not a horse or a bull. The lead needs to be light and comfortable to hold in your hands with no sharp edge to the webbing. A multipoint lead where you can adjust the length of the lead is very useful.

The 15-foot long line is an essential piece of kit for some of the work we'll be doing later on. It will give your dog a choice, and choice is what this training is all about. Have one with a soft woven fabric which won't cut or burn your hands if your dog suddenly zips to the end of it. 1" wide webbing for a larger dog, ¾" for a smaller one, and a handle at the end.

Avoid:

What you do *not* want are extendable leads, bungee leads, anything made with chain, cheap sharp-edged webbing, or a lead less than four feet in length.

Why no extendable lead? These contraptions actually teach the dog to pull! Every time he pulls, he gets more lead. There are also several safety issues around them. I know of cases where the mechanism has broken and the dog has run into the road and been run over. I also know of cases where people have sustained serious burns to their legs or hands - and in one case, their neck - by the cord racing through the mechanism with a heavy speeding dog on the end. And then there are the dogs who panic when the clumpy plastic handle is dropped and bounces along the road behind them as they flee into danger.

The worst thing is that there is no sensitivity or sense of connection through a plastic handle. It may look like a clever idea, but in fact it's a lazy and ineffective option, and totally unsuited for working with a reactive dog.

You have only one chance to make a good first impression

A word about appearances: colours are more important than you may imagine! If the barking dog surging towards you is wearing a red or black harness, you are more likely - according to research into human psychology - to be afraid than if the same dog were wearing a soft pink or turquoise harness. You are more likely to be favourably disposed towards a dog in a pretty flowery collar than one wearing a heavy leather buckled affair with studs. If the owner loves his dog enough to choose pretty colours for him, then there's a chance this dog isn't all bad. Others are therefore less likely to stare at the dog as he walks along the pavement - and staring, as many of you know already, will put a reactive dog on edge. If your dog is a bit butch-looking, or is one of the currently taboo dogs, consider a pretty bandana or a light patterned jacket to present him to the world. Choose dog gear carefully!

People always mistook Lacy as a puppy for a fearsome brown bear cub. And she can look very menacing when in full flow. So she wears a shocking pink collar and harness, and her many leads are all varieties of pink. They'll see her as a pretty girl if it kills me!

Devices used by the Inquisition

By now I hardly need tell you to ditch anything that uses fear or intimidation to get results. So into the bin goes anything you throw at your dog, rattle at her, squirt at her, or anything which uses a battery. *

Please destroy these things - don't pass them to another dog owner!

This is your friend you want to enjoy walks with, not an enemy who has to be kept under control with threats and abuse!

When I've explained how leads and collars work to the owners of a dog I'm working with, I'm always pleased when they tell me they've put all the inappropriate items in the bin - so that no-one in the family can use them again on their family pet.

* This specifically excludes "buzz" vibrating collars for deaf dogs.

Muzzle

Now there's a heated subject! People tend to think that a dog wearing a muzzle must be all bad, and is dangerous. In fact the dog wearing the muzzle is the safest dog, as his armoury is behind closed doors! Sometimes dogs need to wear muzzles because they have a habit of swallowing stones, slugs, or food which makes them ill. The only danger they offer is to themselves. So presuming that a muzzle means a dog is bad is a big mistake.

I can understand you not wanting your barking, lunging, dog to wear a muzzle in case people think she's a dangerous dog. Guess what? They already do! But if there is any history of biting, or just snapping at people, *you* will feel much more relaxed if she's muzzled. As you will learn soon, you being relaxed is a very important part of the training we will be doing. And, of course, if your dog has a bite history - of people, dogs, cats, whatever - it is your duty to protect others and muzzling her is certainly going to do that. Any greyhound that has ever been raced or coursed should always be muzzled when out (as is the law in some countries) to preserve the safety of small fluffy things - be they cats, rabbits, or small dogs.

The first thing to know is that a muzzle can be your friend. If your dog is afraid of people, it's a great way to keep them away! Few people are going to approach your muzzled dog and try to pat her or lean over and stare at her - all big no-no's for the people-reactive dog.

Don't just buy a muzzle and stick it on your dog expecting her to be happy with it. As with the head halter, you need to slowly acclimatise her to love wearing it. You can start with some sort of basket or a paper coffee cup you can cut holes in. Make it a game for her to put her nose into it for a treat! In the Resources section you will find a link to a complete sequence to teach your dog to enjoy wearing a muzzle.

And don't fear that your dog will look nasty. You can get muzzles in pretty colours, and you can attach bows or stickers to them to make them look fun. Lacy's muzzle is black, but has shocking pink bows and ribbons on, to go with her hot pink harness, lead, and collar. Nobody need doubt that she is a girl, and a much-loved pet!

Lacy's pretty muzzle

Choose:

A basket muzzle, which enables your dog to drink, pant, bark, and take treats. If you can find the right toy, they can also pick those up through the bars. A soft rubber muzzle is preferable to a wire muzzle - which can still deliver a mighty bruise when it whacks your leg. The muzzle should fit comfortably round the face, with no pressure under the eyes. It is possible to use a head halter with a muzzle.

Avoid:

A cloth muzzle, or anything that keeps the mouth shut. These are designed for quick application in the vet's surgery, and only for very short lengths of time. The dog is unable to pant. Beware a constricting muzzle on a brachycephalic dog (squashed-nose dog, like a bulldog or pug) - even at the vets. They can't breathe properly - this can end badly.

In this chapter we have learnt that

- Some equipment will help you
- Some equipment will hinder you
- Some equipment should be universally illegal
- We need to face up to the reality of the situation and ensure everyone is safe

Chapter 2
Rewards - what, how, when?

Rewarding your dog with something he really likes is essential to this easy method of training. This may be with a game of chase, tugging with a toy, racing after a ball, being given his dinner bowl, a cuddle, or a tasty treat. It's up to you to find out just what your dog likes (as opposed to what you think he likes) and reward him appropriately when he makes a good choice.

Treats are not a moral issue. They are a means to an end. The end is your dog responding to you and working with you. If employing a few bits of cheese means that my walks are enjoyable and my dog is calm and happy, then that seems a good deal to me. I only give my dogs a treat when they've done something I like: I aim to get through a lot of treats every day!

The treats need to be very tasty - your dog has got to really want them! And you don't want her chewing and chomping on a biscuit for so long that she forgets what she earned it for. So the treat needs to slip down quickly and make your dog think, "Wow! How can I get some more of that?" Your dog needs to know what you like and what does not work with you.

So every time she does something you like, you can mark it by saying, "YES!" and giving her a treat. There is no need for your dog to sit in order to receive a treat. Some dogs think that sitting and begging is the only way to earn a treat, so they sit and beg and annoy at every opportunity. If you are crystal clear about what your dog is doing that is earning the reward (by saying YES), then he will know what actions to repeat, and what doesn't pay. The sitting, begging dog has no idea what causes these random treats to appear.

When you mark an action, you want to mark *as the dog is doing it.* If you are marking a Sit, for instance, you need to say Yes as the bum is going to the floor. If you wait till your dog has already sat, she's now gazing out of the window and thinking of something else. That's not what you want to mark! As the sheepdog trainer John Holmes told us, you need to catch your dog *with his mind down the rabbit-hole,* not wait till he is down the rabbit-hole, when it's too late. You want to catch your dog *thinking* about sitting.

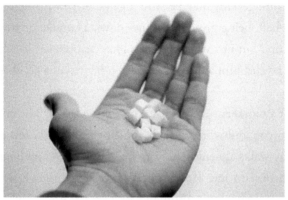

Small, tasty, treats!

Good treats

- Cheese
- Sausage
- Ham
- Chicken
- Frankfurter
- Salami
- Homemade sardine, tuna, or ham cookies
- Freeze-dried 100% meat treats
- Dehydrated liver, heart, lung, etc

…real food in other words. Ideally, they slip down quickly so your dog wants more. Cut them up small - just pea-size will do nicely.

OK treats

- High-quality grain-free commercial treats

Fairly rubbish treats

- Your dog's usual kibble (She gets it anyway. Why should she have to work for it?)
- Cat biscuits
- Dog biscuits
- Stuff of unrecognisable composition sold as pet treats
- Anything you wouldn't put in your own mouth

Do you work more enthusiastically for £60 an hour or for 50p an hour? Quite so. Your dog is the same. Be sure the treats you're offering are worth working for!

How many treats?

It's at this stage that someone usually pipes up and says, "But I don't want to have to bribe my dog. I want him to do it because I say so." Good luck with that, is what I'll respond. Do you get paid to go to work, or do you do it because your boss tells you to? How would you feel if on Friday afternoon your manager said, "You've worked well this week, but I'm not going to bribe you any more so there'll be no pay-check." Would he be seeing you on Monday?

And we're not bribing here. We're rewarding. There really is a big difference. If you wave a treat in front of your dog's nose in order to get his attention, yes - that is a bribe (aka luring). And what do you do if he says "No thanks,

I'd rather carry on chewing your chair leg"? If you can get your dog interacting with you and trying new things to see what will pay, you can reward what you like and ignore what you don't like. And that - you will remember - is the mantra I gave you in Book 1!

Reward what you like
Ignore what you don't like
Manage what you can't ignore

How often do you feed your dog these tasty morsels? That depends on how often you interact with him and how many good responses you can get. There is no time when my dogs may not earn a treat from me, and no place where rewards are not available. So I'm "training" all the time. I prefer to call it conversing or interacting - just like you do with your children. This is real life, not school.

If you're concerned that your dog may gain weight with all these rewards, there are two things you can do. One is to remove an equivalent amount from his dinner bowl, and the other is to use non-food rewards. You want to aim to use non-food rewards *as well as* food ones. Food is very important to all animals, and is the quickest way to teach a lot of new things. You'll also need to teach your dog to enjoy other rewards too: toy play is a big one to encourage.

Of course, if you have a Border Collie he may far prefer toy play as his reward. In that case you'll have to teach him to love treats too, as there are times when play is an inconvenient or inappropriate reward.

You can actually teach this pleasure in both treats and play by giving the less-desired reward, marking with Yes, and immediately following with the favoured reward. You're rewarding your dog for accepting your "inferior" reward. And as you will see as you work with choice training, the cue and the action will become as valuable as the reward that follows. There's fun in store for you!

Start making a list of all the things your dog *loves*. Then highlight all the things he loves that are suitable to be used as a reward. While you're at it, make a note of which he considers the most heavenly reward possible (chasing a toy? a whole sausage?) and which are rather more ordinary rewards - perhaps useful for when you want a slower, more thoughtful, response.

Now when you're in a highly-charged or very distracting situation, you can pull out the heavy artillery. When you're at home and it's quiet, perhaps a lower-value reward will work well. For some dogs, training with dried sprats as rewards is so stimulating that they can completely lose the plot. For others it has to be something as good as a dried sprat to get them to sit up and take notice.

Let your dog tell you what he likes best! If he loves car-rides, then do a moment's training with him just before you grab your keys and take him out to the car. If he loves dozing in a patch of sunshine, you can play some games then open the door to the garden or the south-facing room with the square of sunlight on the floor.

We are different. Our dogs are different. We all learn at different rates. It's up to us to get to know our individual dog and know what makes him tick.

What sort of play?

Play can be anything you and your dog find fun - without any undesirable side-effects such as ripped sleeves and scratched legs. (A licked face is part of the fun.) So for the purposes of this book, I am confining play to fun interaction between owner and dog (as opposed to dog and dog, or dog and toy) which lifts our spirits, causes tails to wag, and builds the bond between us.

The best play simulates one of your dog's instinctive drives. Then you get total immersion in the game - total commitment. All dogs have the same basic instinctive drive: to locate prey, stalk it, chase it, catch it, and kill it. So we'll hijack this sequence to make the best game of all: Tug!

Whatever you've heard about tug being dangerous, giving power to the dog, teaching them to bite, and so on, is all a fallacy. Research (and I mean proper scientific research at a University) has shown that playing tug does not make dogs aggressive. I find the opposite to be the case. If you teach games with lots of impulse control built in, your dog is learning to control herself all the time you are playing. So when you play you teach your dog to grab the toy where you hold it on the floor - not in the air hanging from your hand - to pull as if her life depended on it, to let go when you ask (try holding a piece of cheese to her nostrils for a quick release) and to wait for you to whack the tug on the floor again before grabbing it.

This is a reflection of what they'd learn from their mother when she taught them to hunt. If the pup flies in gung-ho at the first sight of the prey he's likely to stay hungry. A little self-discipline and control will make a hunt fruitful.

A great game for high-speed chasing and catching is a flirt pole. A long, flexible, pole - a carriage whip is perfect - with a soft toy tied to the end of the cord (my current toy is the limb of a teddy bear - "current" because the toy does get shredded) will give hours of fun. Your dog will race like the wind, her sides will be heaving, her eyes will sparkle! And all the while you are teaching her impulse control - how about that!

What's a clicker and do I have to use one?

A clicker is a little gadget you hold in your hand and click to mark the very second your dog is doing something you like. The click is always followed by a treat. It's an excellent way of teaching - especially teaching complex and accurate actions.

But no, you don't need to use one. If you want to work on more complex things like tricks or dance moves, do a bit of reading up on clicker training first to make sure that you do it right. For now, your hands are going to be full enough with lead, treats, and perhaps gloves if it's cold, so don't worry about it.

You should still mark something you like, though! Marking gives the dog the precise information of what it was that earned her a reward and what she needs to do in order to get rewarded again.

Just as effective at indicating your pleasure at what your dog is doing is to say "YES!" enthusiastically. The advantage of a verbal marker is that you'll never leave your voice at home. Say it quickly, at the very instant she does the thing you like. She'll start trying things out to see what makes you say Yes. Now the training is truly interactive.

In this chapter we have learnt that;

- What you reward is what you'll get
- The strength of the reward affects the enthusiasm your dog will deliver
- There are lots of ways to reward your dog for things you like
- A marker word or sound is needed to pinpoint precisely what it is you're rewarding

Chapter 3
Confidence building

Impulse Control

We mentioned impulse control in the last chapter. And there's nothing more empowering than being able to control yourself - and consequently other people and even the situation you find yourself in. Impulse control encourages thoughtfulness, reflection, independence, and builds the ability to make good decisions.

It's what distinguishes the self-centred child from the mature adult. And yes - our dogs can also be mature and make good decisions in the face of great temptation. Think how easy everything else will become when you have a dog who is totally clear about boundaries, is polite and respectful. Think how nice it is when your teenager reaches that stage!

For a deep study of Impulse Control, take a look at the second book in the series **Essential Skills for a Brilliant Family Dog:** *Leave it! How to teach Amazing Impulse Control to your Brilliant Family Dog* which takes you step-by-step through a program to enable you to leave food anywhere in the house in the sure knowledge that it will still be there when you return. It then shows you many other ways your dog can use his new skills to make life easier for you. As you'll expect by now, the methods are all force-free. You'll find more info in the Resources Section.

Responsiveness

In order to have a conversation with someone, they have to be listening. So bleating at your dog who is focussed on something in the distance (on the planet or in his mind) is not going to get you very far. We need our dog to be ready to listen whenever we ask.

So make sure you have got the two games and the Key Lead Skill in Book 1 going well:

Lesson 1: The Precious Name Game
Lesson 2: The Collar Hold
Key Lead Skill no.1: Keeping the lead loose

Don't worry! these also appear in this book in case you missed Book 1. There are a lot more coming in the next chapter, but you need these fluent and fun first.

Tricks!

If your time with your dog is turning into a time of apprehension and worry, there's nothing better to get you both working together - happy and carefree - than to teach a few tricks! There are some great trick training books (see Resources Section) that can get you started. These will build your and your dog's confidence massively. He will enjoy doing something that makes you smile and guarantees a reward. And you can enjoy working with him on something that holds no conflict.

If your dog is people-friendly, he'll like making your friends and visitors smile too! A well-learned trick, like a Sit Pretty, or a Spin, will give your dog something else to do to take his mind off things if he's mildly worried about his environment. Once he's focussed on you and his trick he'll be able to block out the things that are making him anxious.

Isn't this the perfect way to show off your lovely dog! As one student said to me:

> "It's so nice to be able to show that my dog isn't all bad - she just has difficulties in some areas."

ACTION STEP 15:

Choose a very simple trick, teach it at home, then see if you can get it working perfectly everywhere over the next couple of weeks.

Nosework

Dogs' noses, as you probably know, are millions of times more sensitive than our sorry human noses. Let's put those noses to work! Sniffing is a very satisfying canine activity. It lowers the heart-rate and, as you'll remember from Book 1, it is a calming signal to any other dogs around.

So start with simple search games: partially hide a favourite toy - poked under the corner of a carpet, for instance, with part of it sticking out. This minimises the amount of sight being used to find the toy. You'll gradually hide the whole toy in the same place, then moving to different places in the room. Don't be tempted to go from kindergarten to university level in one session! Keep making it easy and fun, and your dog will gradually let his nose take over in the search. You'll hear the vigorous sniffing when that happens!

When you move to the garden, there are a lot more exciting smells out there. There's also weather. Even a slight drift of air can move the scent around a lot, especially in an enclosed area where it will tend to swirl. So go back to the beginning and make it very easy for your dog to succeed. Partially hide the toy under an old flowerpot, for example. Don't hide it in your delicate flowerbed!

Once your dog is good at defaulting to scenting to find things instead of just relying on his eyes, there'll be no more lost balls on walks! And finding hidden children in the house just by scent is always a very popular game: can you imagine the excitement?

You can move on from searching to tracking, where you can lay a strongly-scented track by shuffling along from a start marker for maybe ten yards (fifteen yards if you have a large dog) - lining up with a tree or building in the distance. Show the dog you're placing something between your feet (a favourite toy or large tasty treat), then step out from the track, head back in a big curve, and set off with your dog on a lead or line (preferably connected to a harness). Always be sure you know exactly where the track is - dewy grass or snow is great for this. Only gradually incorporate gentle turns and ordinary strides instead of shuffling.

ACTION STEP 16:

Find out just how clever your dog is by starting some search games with him. Make them hugely exciting and fun. You can play mini search games (toss a toy, or just a stick or fir cone that you've handled, into the long grass) when you're out and about which will help him to keep his mind off the things that worry him, by giving him a job to do.

Distance

And here comes the big one!

Whenever your dog is unhappy about a situation, the first thing to do is make distance.

(This should be in flashing lights and accompanied by sirens and awoogas.)

You need to be working at a distance at which your dog can cope. So if you see a dog or a black plastic sack up ahead - whatever worries your dog - and she is getting twitchy about it, turn and back up a bit. Maybe 10 yards, maybe 50 yards. "Can you look at it from here?" you can ask her. Get to a place where she can view the hazard without stress, and is able to switch her focus easily to you when asked. Then you can consider moving closer. Maybe 1 yard closer, maybe 5 yards - "Can you look at it from here?"

You will be able to establish a distance at which your dog can view the "trigger" (the thing that sets her off) so you know where to start from. This distance can vary, of course, depending on the severity of the threat, whether it's advancing towards you, whether it's making a noise, whether it's moving fast, whether it's windy, what you had for breakfast - and so on. But it gives you a starting point. Gradually the "safe" distance will become automatic for you. You'll be able to gauge how far you need to be from this particular trigger on this particular day.

You'll be able to turn with a cheery "Let's go!" and head away. In calm and quiet. What bliss!

If you were terrified of spiders, would it help to have to walk through a whole lot of them - on the ground, dangling from bushes, flying on the breeze in front of you? Would you trust the person who is trying to force you to "face your fear"? Would you not feel much happier if you could make a choice to turn away as soon as you see all those spiders? This is what you'll be doing for your dog. Your aim will be a calm dog - nothing more.

Personal space

We all have a "personal space" into which only very familiar people may venture. If a stranger approaches you and stands right in front of your face you are going to feel very uncomfortable. You'll most likely take a step back. You may avoid giving them direct eye contact in case it encourages them. You could feel agitated and keen to move on.

On the other hand, if a stranger approaches you with a brief soft-eyed glance and smile, averts their gaze, slows down as they approach, stops a couple of yards from you and shifts their bodyweight back, you will feel much less threatened.

Your dog is the exact same! Only his personal space is way bigger. If I were walking my (reactive) dog and saw you and your dog coming towards us, and I wanted to ask the way to the station, I'd stop way further back than I would if we were both dogless. That may be five yards, or ten yards if it's not too crowded and noisy and I can call out my request to you.

If I were to come to a comfortable position for two strangers without dogs to meet - maybe three yards - this would be much, much too close for my dog, and perhaps yours too. While attending to your answer, I would be failing to notice my dog - who could be going through her entire repertoire of calming signals. As the other dog doesn't move away (because he can't) and I don't move her away (because I'm not paying attention) there may be a sudden flurry and noise from down there at pavement level.

Get used to the fact that your dog's safe distance from a stranger or threat is miles bigger than our safe distance. Make allowances, and keep her calm!

Something new appears near us

This has a fancy name - Sudden Environmental Change. It just means that something new has appeared and it may alarm your dog. It will especially alarm any of the guard, guardian, or herding breeds, who have been bred to notice anything that shouldn't be there. We looked at this early on in Book 1.

If you have a reactive dog you'll become accustomed to "sweeping" the environment to check for UXBs (that's "unexploded bombs" for those of you who watch different tv programs from me!). You'll be looking for whatever your dog is known to react to - dogs, only black dogs, only running dogs, people in hats, all people … etc, and you'll also get into the habit of checking for sudden new things. This could be somebody walking behind you and catching up with you. It could be a pile of garbage left out for the binmen. Or a dog suddenly appearing up ahead.

I'll be giving you techniques to defuse these UXBs quickly and quietly. But you have to notice them first! We're taller than our dogs, so we tend to see things first. If you can notice and act accordingly, you can forestall a reaction. Your dog's confidence will grow when he's not endlessly getting frights.

One thing after another

This is something that can unnerve any of us. Picture this: you're in the kitchen preparing dinner - in a bit of a rush as one of the family needs to go out. You've got everything nicely under control when the phone rings. As you dry your hands and head for the phone, there's an urgent knock and shout at the door. Caught between the two, you hear your pan boiling over! Whoever you speak to next is likely to be snapped at!

This is known in the trade as "Trigger Stacking". You could cope with the rushed meal preparation. At any other time you could cope with a phone call, or a knock at the door. But all at once is too much!

This may account for the big puzzle of why your dog barks at something one day and passes it by at other times. Maybe he sees a dog in the distance, then he hears someone shout over to his left - just behind him a screaming child is approaching on a bike: boom! - it's all too much. He doesn't know what to do so he does his best to keep them all away from him in the only way he knows: barking, shrieking, lunging, bouncing ...

ACTION STEP 17:

So here is a new mantra for you (not quite so new if you read Book 1- but its huge importance makes it totally worth repeating and emphasising here):

Show your dog that he never has to meet another person or dog in his life.

Yes - one day he may want to. But for now, we are not going to put him through this trauma. So when you see ahead of you something that is likely to upset your dog, you wait till he's clocked it, give a cheery "Let's go!" and head off in another direction. What relief your dog will experience! What trust will she put in you now! What a confidence-builder this is!

Responsibility

While you are working on helping your dog overcome her fears you have a huge responsibility to keep everyone else safe.

ACTION STEP 18:

If your dog has a bite history, or you fear losing control of your dog and think he may bite, there is no off-lead exercise for him outside your property or a private fenced area, and he must wear a muzzle when out. More on how to achieve this in upcoming chapters.

In this chapter we have learnt that

- Building your dog's confidence in herself - as well as in you - is key
- There are lots of ways we can do this
- Distance is of critical importance
- Distance comes in many shapes and sizes
- It's up to us to ensure our dog cannot inflict damage

Chapter 4
Let's get cracking!

Lead Skills

You may think that the lead is there to control your dog. You may have been told that you need to control your dog, to make him do things, and to forcibly prevent him from doing other things. But as you'll remember from Book 1, we are not working that way!

What we are doing is giving the dog a choice. Being able to exercise a choice allows your dog a measure of independence which he needs in order to be able to make good choices in the future.

When dressing a small child, a lot of conflict can be avoided by saying, "Would you like to wear your red jumper or your blue jumper?" Note that there's no mention of fairy princess dresses, superman outfits, or … nothing at all. You have already narrowed her options down to what you would like her to wear today. So you don't care which way she chooses. When your toddler decides which jumper she's going to wear she'll stick to that decision because she made it! Being presented with a straight choice simplifies the task for her and teaches her how to analyse problems and come to a conclusion.

Similarly, when your dog is on the lead and he pulls ahead: instead of yanking the lead and hauling the dog back beside you, you stand still and offer the dog a choice. "Would you like to come back here, or would you rather stand still all day?" You know you can outwait your dog, so you don't mind which way he chooses. After a bit of resistance your dog will work out how to get you moving again and slide back into position. I'm assuming you've already taught him where he should be when you're walking! If not, take a look at the third book in the **Essential Skills for a Brilliant Family Dog** series: *Let's Go! Enjoy Companionable Walks with your Brilliant Family Dog,* which you'll find in the Resources section.

Changing *your* view of the lead is the first thing to do. Your dog may be a determined puller on the lead. This pulling has nothing to do with trying to rule you! Dogs like to get places faster than our miserable slowcoach speed, and if fear is added to this, they'll want to go even faster.

Our necks vs their necks

As we saw in Chapter 1 (the very first thing you learnt in this book!) physiologically, our necks are virtually identical to dogs' necks. So a force tightening on your dog's neck or pressing against his throat is going to have a similar effect on him as it would on us.

Not only do you want to avoid the pain this involves on a dog who is pulling on his lead, but it's essential to remove the anxiety associated with this pressure in order to help your reactive dog view the world with equanimity. So the first step is to use a non-aversive harness (see Chapter 1 and the Resources section) and a comfortable lead of at least 6 feet in length, and the second step is to learn how to use the lead effectively and kindly to get the best possible results.

So your lead is not for yanking or pulling your dog around. The lead is a connection between you, and at the same time a way to stop your dog running into trouble. I'm going to show you a total of six **Key Lead Skills**. Once you know these and you've assimilated them into your daily interaction with your dog you'll wonder how you ever managed without them! I suggest you bookmark this page (that's easy to do on an e-book!) and learn one at a time, coming back for the next one when you've mastered the first.

It may surprise - nay, astonish! - you to learn that if you keep the lead loose, your dog will keep it loose too. Really! It takes two to tango, as the saying goes, and it takes two to have a tight lead. One of us has to stop pulling, and as we're the ones with the bigger brains, it needs to be us.

Your anxious dog's reactivity is going to be massively increased by pulling into her lead. Let's start the change.

You never have to pull your dog's lead again!

Here's an exercise for you to change this entirely. You will recognise it from Book 1. You needed to learn this one as soon as possible, but I'm also including it here so you have all the Key Lead Skills in the same place for easy reference. You can learn this skill in the kitchen first, then graduate to the garden before trying it on the road.

Key Lead Skill No.1
Holding the Lead

1. Have your dog on a longish lead (at least 2 metres)
2. Stand still and let the dog pull to the end of the lead, wherever she wants to go
3. Keep your hand close to your hip. Tuck your thumb into your belt if necessary
4. Wait. Wait till the lead slackens the tiniest bit. It doesn't matter why. You may think you'll need to wait forever, but it's usually only 20 seconds or so at most
5. As soon as you feel the lead relax - for any reason at all, don't judge - call your dog happily and reward her with a tasty treat at your knee
6. Repeat till she understands that it's up to her to keep the lead loose

This exercise is simplicity itself. It tells your dog that you are no longer the one that's pulling. Your hands are soft. It's her choice if she pulls. Given a little time, she'll choose not to pull at all.

If your dog is in the habit of lurching to the end of the lead as soon as it's on, you may have to repeat this exercise frequently. In most cases we need repeat it only long enough to get the new system of lead-holding into our own heads. Once we've got it, our dog will get it.

Remember, dogs are doers, not not-doers. So your dog is learning to keep the lead loose, rather than not to pull on it. See the difference?

What you accept is what you get

Every time you put the lead on your dog, you need to remember to keep your hand close to you and wait for *her* to slacken the lead. If you are in the habit of putting on the lead and letting your dog pull you to the door, then that is what will happen.

What you reward is what you get

There are few better rewards for most dogs then heading out through that door! Your dog needs to learn that - no matter what happened in the past - things have now changed, which means pulling on the lead will get her nowhere. Dogs aren't dumb. They do what works.

From now on you will never move until the lead is slack. NEVER! If you find your arm floating out, recapture it and tuck it into your belt! If it keeps happening, put one of your children on "arm-watch." They'll love having the chance of pointing out your mistake to you!

Time to keep still

Once your dog has learnt to keep that lead loose, and stay more or less near you, you can start on the next Key Lead Skill. It's incredibly useful and keeps your dog calmly under control without any effort from either of you. If you want to stop and chat to someone, make a purchase in a shop, or wait at a bus stop, you can put the handbrake on and park your dog. This is a great way to immobilise your dog without any vestige of force or anger. And it removes from your reactive dog the need to be on duty, watching, guarding, worrying. This is how you do it:

Key Lead Skill No.2
Parking

1. The first thing is to hold your dog's collar. Rather than waving your arm about trying to catch the collar on a leaping dog, simply run your hand down the lead till you reach the collar, and slip a finger under it.
2. While holding the collar (gently!), allow the lead to fall to the floor and stand on it right beside your dog's front paw, hanging on to the handle all the while.
3. Now you can let go of the collar, straighten up, and keep holding on to that handle. A 6-foot lead is ideal for this.
4. Ignore your dog. No more interaction between you.

Your dog can take any position she likes. She's simply unable to pull or jump up. Your hands are free to delve into your purse or drink a coffee. Passers-by are safe from being jumped on. Your dog will find that as nothing more is happening, sitting or lying down is a good option. Your anxious dog can relax, knowing that nothing more is expected of her.

When you get fluent and quick at parking, you'll have a way to anchor your dog easily. Be sure to hold the collar before trying to stand on the lead or you'll find yourself doing the can-can as your dog flies forward as you try to get your foot on a waving lead!

Keeping your hands soft

Keeping your hands soft on a floppy lead can be hard to do. You've spent ages holding the lead tight as if your life depended on it, restricting your dog's freedom. This is understandable as you may have been afraid he would hurt someone.

But now we want the dog to have freedom - freedom to choose to stay calm! - so making sure you keep your hands soft and the lead loose is going to go a long way towards this. If your dog sails off away from you, you need to be able to stop him without yanking him off his feet. You want him to slow down, turn, and choose to come back to you. The lead needs to stay fluid so nothing sudden happens. Your anxious grasp when you clutch the lead tight and the tension this causes will tell your dog that something bad is happening. Perhaps he'd better bark at the nearest thing to keep it away!

I know you're thinking that if you loosen the lead, he'll pull all the time - but that's the old thinking. You now know that giving your dog the freedom to choose and then rewarding the choice you want will have him making good decisions in no time. As he learns these new skills, things will be changing dramatically before your eyes. Remember to choose a quiet area to practice - you can't teach these new skills in the middle of the park or a busy shopping street!

Holding the handle safely and flaking the line

Whatever lead you are using (and please don't use one less than 6 feet in length!) you need to hold it safely. Safe so that your hand can't slip out, and safe so that your wrist can't get broken if your dog suddenly lurches out at an angle. I am right-handed and have given the instructions for a right-hander. Use whichever hand feels comfortable for you.

Key Lead Skill No.3a
Holding the handle safely

1. Hold the lead handle up in one hand - say, your left hand - while the other hand - your right hand - goes through the loop like threading a needle
2. Then, while the handle is round your right wrist, bring the lead up and grip it against your right hand with your right thumb.
3. The line is now emerging from between your thumb and hand. This way you have a secure hold without stress, and your bones are safe!
4. Your other hand will be a channel for the line to run through loosely to your dog.

If this has totally confused you (sorry), you will be pleased to know that there is a video illustrating this and the following lead skills which you'll find in the Resources section.

Long line skills

For a lot of the training you'll be learning, you'll need to use a long line. Panic not! It's very easy when you know how. I find that people - once introduced to the joys of the long line - never want to go back to a short lead, except, of course, on the street.

This long line is not going to trail on the ground - it's going to stay in your hands, free of mud and wet, and is not going to wind your dog's legs up in knots or be a trip hazard for you or any passing children. You can watch the video in the Resources section, and I'll describe it for you here too.

A long line of about 15 feet is perfect for our purposes - see Chapter 1 of this book. It will provide a connection between you and your dog while allowing her to mooch around in a natural manner, and - importantly - give her the freedom to express her body language. You will always have a safe hold of the handle (and a lot of the line) but you can allow your dog to make choices. Don't worry, we'll make sure these are all good choices! Just like the red or blue jumper offered to your toddler, we will limit the range of choices she can make, and weight the best choice heavily in our favour.

So the first thing to learn is how to control that line without breaking your fingers, or causing your dog to be yanked to a halt. This system is known by the nautical term "flaking" - used when the line is laid out on the deck in figures of eight, or snaked. This ensures that when the net is thrown overboard, the line runs freely and there is no danger of a knot stopping the net from deploying, or of a coil catching a sailor's leg and taking him overboard with it.

You may be in the habit of winding a rope up in loose coils. The danger of this is that if your dog suddenly shoots forward, a coil will close round your fingers. There is a very real danger of breaking a finger this way!

Key Lead Skill No.3b
Flaking the line

1. Layer your line, in the hand holding the handle, in long bows or figures of eight.
2. As your dog moves away, you can open your fingers for the line to snake out through the channel your other hand is making, then as you and your dog near each other again,
3. you can flake it into your hand again so it's not touching the ground.

All these lead skills really become very easy with a bit of practice - even for people who have difficulty distinguishing left and right, or who are not very nimble-handed. The long line will become a soft and relaxed connection between you and your dog. It will shrink and grow organically as your dog moves closer to you then further away again. It's like gently holding a child's hand, rather than gripping that hand tight as you might if you were near a busy road with a fractious four-year-old.

Whoa there!

So let's look now at how you can slow your dog to a gentle halt without pulling. You really never have to pull your dog's lead again!

Key Lead Skill No. 4
Slow Stop

1. Your dog is heading away from you, perhaps in pursuit of a good scent, or trying to reach someone.
2. As he moves away, loosely cup your left hand under the lead, letting the line run through freely, gradually closing your grip so he can feel this squeezing action as the lead slows down.
3. This will slow him sufficiently to ease him into a stand.
4. Now relax your hands and lead - you may need to take a small step forward to let your hands soften and drop down - and admire your dog standing on a loose lead.
5. You can attract him back to your side if you need to with your voice - treat, and carry on.

This should all be calm, mostly noiseless, and easy. It's like holding your friend's hand and gently slowing them down till they come back into step beside you. No need for "Oi!" "Stop!" "C'me 'ere" or anything else other than saying, "Good Boy!" and giving him a welcoming smile when he reorients to you.

Try this first with another person instead of your dog to help you. Ask them to hold the clip of the lead in their hand, turn away from you and let the lead drape over their shoulder, with you behind them holding the line. As they walk away and you start to close the fingers of your left hand on the lead, they should be fully aware of that sensation and respond to it. They'll be able to tell you very clearly if you're gently slowing them or jolting them to a stop! Your dog too will recognise this feeling on the lead as "Oh hallo, we're stopping now."

When you start, it may take a few attempts to get your dog to stay still and balanced when she stops so that you're able to relax the lead. After a while she'll know that this rubbing sensation on the lead is the precursor to a halt. The right sort of harness will help enormously to get her to balance on her own four feet instead of using you as a fifth leg. See the Resources section at the end of the book.

You may find that your dog slows beautifully to a halt, but as soon as you relax your line she surges forward again! So when you slow stop her, relax your hands just a little (an inch or so) to test whether she's standing balanced on her own feet. If she immediately starts to lean forward again, don't move, but ease her to a stop again - maybe just using your fingers on the line - and test again. Sooner or later, she's going to realise that slow stop means stand still. The point to remember is that if you've decided she should stop (you may be seeing trouble up ahead) then stop she shall. Don't move yourself once you've committed to stopping.

But what if stopping is not enough?

There are going to be times when you can slow stop your dog, but she is still trying to surge forward. Maybe you're just too close to the thing that's worrying her. So, as you know from Chapter 3 of this book:

Whenever your dog is unhappy about a situation, the first thing to do is make distance.

But how can you do that? You know that if you try and haul her back when she's this aroused that it's going to turn into an ugly mess. Not only is it hard to drag her backwards - her feet are firmly planted behind her and you're pulling against her strongest muscles, in her back and haunches (think of a horse drawing a cart) - but worse, just trying to pull her back may trigger an outburst.

You are going to love this lead skill! Instead of trying to force her to comply with what you want, remember the red and blue jumpers: give her a choice!

Always allow time for a choice

Key Lead Skill No.5
Stroking the line

1. Hold onto the line and stay put yourself to make sure your dog can't move forward
2. With a hand-over-hand action, *gently stroke* the line as you make attractive cooing and kissy noises (you are *not* pulling the lead).
3. Your dog will feel this feathery touch and turn to look at you, as you bend over behind her in a kind of play-bow inviting her to join you.
4. She'll turn of her own volition and trot happily towards you, the scary thing quite forgotten.
5. Back up a few steps while she engages her eyes with yours, then you can turn and head away.

It's as easy as that. It is a joy! And people are usually astonished when they learn this skill. Make sure you have the other skills down before you start on this one.

Most of you will have some experience with children, either through having your own, or through having been one. Think of the times you've wanted to distract your child - possibly from a dangerous situation - by saying "Is that a *giraffe* over there?" or some such. You get a lightning response! This is the same kind of idea we're using here. Distraction and diversion and a lightness of voice.

All these lead skills can be done with a short or a long line. I find that it's easier to learn the first two on a short line, and the next three on a long line. Once you've mastered them, you can use them with any lead.

It's you who has to do some learning here. Just like driving a car, if you grate the gears and stamp on the pedals your car is not going to perform well. To get a smooth "drive" with your dog, you're going to need to learn these Key Lead Skills carefully. Your dog will say, "Oh, that's what she wants!" and it will all become a breeze. You really will wonder how you managed before!

In this chapter we've learnt that

- The lead is a lovesome thing that forms a connection between you and your dog
- There's no need to haul your dog about
- You never have to pull your dog's lead again!
- Choice is the name of the game

Section 2

Choice Training

Chapter 5
Why Choice Training?

As we've seen, Choice Training is empowering to dogs. It's empowering to people too, and is the more enlightened way to educate children, both at home and at school. If you can involve the subject in their own education/training, they have the ability to decide things for themselves instead of having things done *to* them.

You may be thinking that if you give your dog a choice she'll automatically choose the wrong one. But that's where a bit of clever setting up can help weight her choices in our favour. Remember those red and blue jumpers, where you didn't care which one was chosen, but you didn't offer the fairy outfit?

Choice Training is the method used for successful training of guide dogs for the blind, seizure alert dogs, dogs for the disabled, search and rescue dogs, dogs for PTSD sufferers, and the like. Even police dogs are now beginning to be trained in a humane way that honours the dog, and there are some notable trailblazers in this field (see the Appreciation page).

Not only can dogs learn these useful skills to help mankind, but they can do them for the sheer enjoyment! Take dancing with dogs, dog tricks, dressage for dogs (aka Obedience competition), agility, flyball, not to mention picking things up for you at home, fetching the lead, finding your phone …

Then there are the truly astonishing feats! Not only have dogs been taught to drive a car, but they have also flown a plane in tricky manoeuvres. See the

Resources section if you don't believe me! Watch some of the footage of these achievements - using abandoned dogs from shelters - and you'll never dismiss your dog's intelligence again! All this is done fastest with Choice Training.

Handling

Many reactive dogs are sensitive in other areas too. So touch sensitivity and sound sensitivity may need to be addressed.

ACTION STEP 19:

Revisit the **Collar Hold game**, featured in Book 1 and again in Chapter 1 of this book. It's fundamental that you should be able to slide a hand easily into your dog's collar and achieve connection and calm. If you haven't done this exercise yet, *do it now!*

Treating touch sensitivity is a similar process - light touch, feed treat; light touch, feed treat - as you touch different parts of your dog's body, using different pressure (sometimes a feather touch, sometimes a press, sometimes a soft squeeze, e.g. of the paw). Be sure that you are not holding the treat to the dog's nose *while* you touch him. If you do that he will be focussed so closely on the treat that he may not even notice you touching him - which defeats the object of the exercise! We want him to be fully aware, but tolerant and not fearful. The essence of this method is to work in short sessions (maybe one minute long) and only very gradually up the ante. You don't leap from a soft touch of the face into a close examination of his back teeth!

If a particular spot is a no-go area for your dog, go and get that thorough vet check! If there's intermittent buried pain your vet may struggle to locate it in a dog who is tense and anxious under examination and not giving anything away. This is where you will have success with a canine massage therapist who can relax the dog before delving into their bodies. See Book 1, and the Resources section. *I'd* be snappy if anyone touching *me* sparked off a searing pain.

Remember that an abnormally aggressive response to touch, especially in a sleeping dog, needs a thorough vet check for pain or other neurological cause.

Is it you that's causing the pain?

The key here is that your dog will associate *something* with any pain or discomfort he's feeling. That something he's latched on to may be the approach of a person holding a broom. It may be entering the vet's surgery. It may be being manhandled so you can reach his claws. So if you have to administer a treatment which may be uncomfortable, it's a good idea to get him to associate something else with this pain, and not you!

There are various techniques about that focus on the dog giving you permission to treat him - having him become a party to his own treatment. Picture this: you go to the dentist for your appointment. While you're talking to the receptionist, the dentist creeps up on you, grabs your jaw and forces it open to poke instruments in. Horror! This is an assault! And yet isn't this what people often do to their dogs?

A better scenario would be that you go into the dentist's surgery. He indicates *The Chair*. Now when you get into that chair you are effectively giving the dentist permission to open your mouth and start poking about in there. It's just as unpleasant as before - but this time you gave your consent.

So get your dog to give you consent by transferring the "this may hurt" feelings onto something else. Some people use a pot of treats on the floor. As long as the dog sits or lies still in front of that pot he'll be given a treat. Gradually you can pick up a paw or start brushing a tail while you dish out the treats. If your dog leaps up and flees, let him. When he ventures back he can choose to station himself in front of the treat pot again. He's saying, "Ok, you can brush me now". You could also get out the implements he's worried about - the nail clippers or the claw-grinder, and perhaps use a particular mat for him to sit on, which you only use for treatments. When he comes to you, you can reward him for his bravery. He knows what's going to happen - you're not going to jump him.

If you call your dog over for a cuddle then grab him and swing him over onto his back so you can check his tangles, how's he going to feel next time you call him?

Choice, choice, choice! Think of that dentist and let your dog have a say in his own care.

That's my name!

The biggest area of conflict around choice may well be the recall. Your dog is off gallivanting about, rolling in who-knows-what, playing with other dogs or chasing a bunny trail, and you call him. Now he has a choice! Does he ignore you, or come barrelling in to you just to experience your delight with him? The recall warrants a whole book to itself, and in fact it has one - the fourth book in the series **Essential Skills for a Brilliant Family Dog:** *Here Boy! Step-by-step to a Stunning Recall from your Brilliant Family Dog.* More info in the Resources section.

But you can make a start, right there where you're reading this. Say your dog's name. Did he perk up, open his eyes, prick his ears, give a slow thud of his tail, even come over to you? Any of those responses is a good one and warrants a treat. Be sure you only ever use your dog's name when you can pair it with something good (see **Lesson 1: The Precious Name Game** in Book 1). I'll show you again here, as it's critically important that your dog thinks his name is wonderful and always worth responding to. We expect a lot – we need to build.in the response we want before taking it for granted.

ACTION STEP 20:

Lesson 1: The Precious Name Game revisited

1. Say dog's name cheerily whenever you notice him
2. When he responds - by raising an eyebrow or hurtling towards you and crashing into your legs - reward him with something good
3. Repeat at every opportunity throughout the day
4. Enjoy your dog

Your reward may be a treat, putting his lead on for a walk (if walks are enjoyable), opening the door to the garden, playing a game, and so on.

In this chapter we have learnt that:

- Giving your dog a choice will result in better decisions from her
- You can extend this choice-making to letting her participate in her own care
- Her first choice should be to respond automatically to her name

Chapter 6
Is this all woolly ideas or is there real science behind it?

If facts and figures are anathema to you, skip to the next chapter. But if the nuts and bolts of human and animal behaviour interest you - why we actually do what we do - then read on. References are in the Resources section.

Looking first at specifically dog-focussed scientific work, the two pillars are Pavlov, the originator of Classical Conditioning, and B.F. Skinner, whose pioneering work with a broad range of animals resulted in Operant Conditioning being shown to be the best way to train any animal. We're animals too.

Pavlov's Dogs and Classical Conditioning

Classical Conditioning was first described by Ivan Pavlov (1849-1936). This area of study came as a by-product of his pioneering work on the human digestive system for which he won a Nobel Prize in 1904. His work was far-reaching and forms the basis of what we know about digestion today.

But his name has been linked in the popular mind with one thing only – Pavlov's Dogs. In his study of the purpose and function of saliva, Pavlov used dogs in his laboratory. They were kept immobile, with drains collecting the saliva through fistulae in the dogs' necks. The objective was to collect the saliva for analysis when the dogs were fed. It was soon discovered, however, that the dogs would begin salivating increasingly earlier in the food preparation chain - first the sight of the lab technicians, then just the sound of human activity, became enough to get the juices flowing in anticipation of their food.

Pavlov's genius was in interrupting this chain with a specific, non-food-linked sound. Amongst others, he chose his famous bell. The bell was rung before feeding, and after a few exposures, the dogs would begin to salivate at the sound of the bell - regardless of the time or other factors – and in the absence of food. Pavlov had effectively put the salivation (an unconditioned or spontaneous, unconsidered response) under stimulus control. Put another way, the bell cued the drooling. So by using a hitherto neutral stimulus (the bell) he could cause the salivation to occur without the normal, natural, unconditioned stimulus of the presence of food. The association that the bell signified food meant the bell would cue the drooling in the absence of food.

How does this apply to us?

With your own dog, you'll be able to see many examples of Classical Conditioning at work:

- Barking at the doorbell
- Leaping up at the sound of the car keys or when seeing you pick up the lead
- Appearing at your feet when you bang the dog bowl
- Rapt attention at the sound of the fridge door opening,
- or a plastic bag rustling,
- or the cat flap opening!

These sights or sounds all stimulate a response of excitement or salivation, even without the expected result of a visitor at the door, going for a walk, dinner, or the entry of the cat. This response has developed through continual repetition of a sequence which the dog now anticipates.

You can see now where some of your dog's more annoying habits have come from, and how you can change them! Control the stimulus (the thing that's causing the reaction) and you control the outcome. In fact, if you remove the stimulus entirely - disconnect the doorbell, for instance - you can completely eliminate that response. Think about that!

Operant Conditioning

Operant Conditioning is the name given to the shaping system first described by B.F. Skinner (1904-1990) in 1938 in *The Behavior of Organisms*.

Skinner was influenced by Pavlov. Working largely with rats and pigeons, Skinner's work had a far-reaching effect on education and psychology. From a practical standpoint, it was used extensively in the American war effort in the forties. Dolphins were used for underwater work where it was unsafe for divers, and chickens became ace spotters - of life rafts in a choppy ocean far below the rescue plane - and of bombing targets.

It was developed and refined by the dolphin trainers who, after World War II, turned their attention to training animals for aquarium displays. The dolphin trainers introduced a marker. It's impossible to get a fish to a dolphin at the high point of a jump, so they marked the moment with a whistle, signalling the correct response from the animal and the imminent arrival of a fish. This whistle is a Secondary Reinforcer.

- A Primary Reinforcer is something that the subject finds innately reinforcing, such as food, play, or social interaction.

- A Secondary Reinforcer is found rewarding by the subject by its association with a Primary Reinforcer, for example money, tokens, whistle, clicker, or a marker word - "Yes!"

Operant Conditioning is so called because the subject has to decide to do something to achieve a reward - to operate on its environment. In Classical

Conditioning, an action which occurs naturally is paired with a stimulus or cue. For example, offering your hand for the dog to touch: the dog comes to sniff your hand, then you add the cue to the hand-touching action. This cue could be a word, or simply offering your hand. In Operant Conditioning the animal can make a choice of what behaviour to offer.

In a "Skinner Box" - a small chamber for testing the responses of animals, often equipped with a food-producing mechanism - rats or pigeons could sleep, groom, run around, or press a lever which delivered food - a Primary Reinforcer. Skinner introduced Pavlov's discoveries by pairing a stimulus to the food delivery, so the subjects knew that touching the lever produced food. Naturally, touching the lever became very popular! When Skinner stopped rewarding the lever-pressing by failing to deliver food, after a flurry of repeated attempts and frustration the action died out entirely – that's known as an Extinction Burst.

Picture the angry toddler demanding an ice cream: he will get louder and noisier until (if unrewarded) … eventually he gives up.

Why does this matter to me and my pet dog?

The possibilities opened up by Operant Conditioning extend far beyond simply achieving a desired action. It has become a window into the animal's mind. Daily, we are extending our knowledge of how the critters think. The practical applications are boundless: in dogs alone we have mine detection, search and rescue, dogs for the disabled, hearing dogs for the deaf, seeing dogs for the blind, seizure alert medical assistance dogs, companion dogs, entertaining dogs, dancing dogs, agility dogs. A lot of the things these dogs can do would be very difficult, if not impossible, to teach by force, by luring, or by moulding the action - and there would be no enthusiasm and joy in the task!

Skinner's pioneering work, followed up and expanded by Marion Breland, Bob Bailey, and Karen Pryor amongst others, has enabled dogs to be used in so many of these new applications.

The important thing to remember with Operant Conditioning is that what you reinforce is what you get, so the timing of the reward is crucial! One moment you think you are capturing a wonderful Sit Pretty, but because you were too slow with your marker, you actually reinforced a floppy Sit. Remember the dolphins jumping: your marker means a reward is on its way. Clarity is key!

A word about punishment

Operant Conditioning has its own clearly defined language - Reinforcement or Punishment, Positive or Negative - which can confuse people as it may not mean the same as is popularly perceived.

- Positive means adding or starting something
- Negative means taking something away or stopping it
- Reinforcement means to encourage what you want by rewarding it, making it more likely to happen again
- Punishment refers to punishing the behaviour, not the animal, making the action less likely to happen again. It does not necessarily include traditional punishments such as beating.

Put very briefly:

- Positive Reinforcement = Good starts
- Positive Punishment = Bad starts
- Negative Reinforcement = Bad stops
- Negative Punishment = Good stops

These are known as the Four Quadrants.

But you don't need to remember all this - *just aim for Positive Reinforcement and reward what you like!*

If your dog does something you like, for instance, and you turn away and ignore her, this is punishing - discouraging the action. Imagine walking down the street, spotting someone you know, giving a cheery smile, and your acquaintance turns his head sharply away to walk past you without a word. How would you feel? What would you do next time you saw him on the street?

Skinner proved that if an action is rewarded, the subject is likely to repeat that action. Similarly, if an action is punished, the subject is unlikely to repeat it. How many times did you have to put your hand into the steam from a kettle before you stopped doing it? There is fallout from punishment, however, that eliminates its use from any humane training program. Obviously it causes unhappiness and pain, which should render it unacceptable to civilised people, but it also causes distrust, alienation, lying, and deceitful behaviour. If a child has been smacked for stealing a cake, he's going to make very sure he doesn't get caught while stealing the next one! It doesn't necessarily stop what you don't want - it may drive it underground.

Repeatedly rewarding what you *do* like will work much, much faster, and your dog's response will be durable - she'll always make the right choice. It is the element of choice that will transform your relationship with your dog, and - secret tip! - it works just the same with children, spouses, and work colleagues!

Think of the joy of never administering a telling-off ever again!

Impulse Control

There is plenty of scientific proof concerning the principles of instant versus delayed gratification in humans, and it appears to me that it works just the same in your dog.

Sigmund Freud, back in 1911, argued that deferred gratification was a marker of increased maturity. Then Walter Mischel conducted his Marshmallow Test experiments at Stanford University in the late 1960s, on children between ages three and five. In the Marshmallow Test, a child had to choose between eating one favourite treat straight away, or - if they could wait for 15 minutes - be rewarded with two treats. A small number of the children caved in straight away and settled for one treat. Of the remainder who chose to wait, only one third managed to last out the fifteen minutes and earn their double reward.

One of the findings was that if the researcher interacting with the child appeared inconsistent and broke promises, the child would lose faith in the new game and just take his one marshmallow while he could. This provides an interesting insight into our need as parents and dog-owners to be consistent and reliable - however busy or stressed we may be!

The detailed follow-up studies over the next 40 years were revealing. The children who, at 4, were able to delay gratification did better in school and university, were more successful, and enjoyed a more healthy lifestyle. The ability to make good choices is a predictor of a person's ability to make the best of their life. They can choose rational behaviour over desires - the pre-frontal cortex over the limbic system.

Cognitive Behavioural Therapy uses the "if-then" framework to help people overcome unwanted desires. "If this happens, then I move into that strategy." Repetition leads to new habits being formed.

So while the ability to control impulses in the face of food does not directly impinge on your dog's fearfulness, it is something that he can apply to the actions he takes, and will hugely help him to move into strategies that will work for him in the future. Essentially, dogs do what works. And we are going to give him techniques that will work better than his current knee-jerk reaction of barking and lunging at something he fears.

How empowering this is for your dog!

In this Chapter you've learnt that:

- The research into the dog's mind is very advanced
- How you can adapt this knowledge for you and your pet
- People and dogs are much the same
- "It's all Greek to me," says your dog

Chapter 7
An introduction to Choice Training

Let's get into how Choice Training works.

1. Catch your dog doing something right

If you are ignoring your dog when he's quiet and affable, and as soon as he puts a paw out of line you come down on him like a ton of bricks, you are teaching him to focus on the thing you don't like. And all the time he was doing something you *do* like, it was not being noted or admired!

You want to switch this around. Your training mantra (which I gave you in Book 1) is:

Reward what you like
Ignore what you don't like
Manage what you can't ignore

To begin with, you may find this very hard! But this slots very well into All-Day Training. Rather than having formal training sessions with your dog, regard every interaction as a training session. You don't want your dog to *perform on cue*, so much as just be. And his just being is what you want to focus on.

If you don't give him a choice, it'll be pot luck whether he ever works out what you want. Giving him a choice, showing him that his actions affect outcomes, gives him a responsibility that he will grow into. This will change your relationship for both of you. Rather than a master-robot relationship, you will have a friend-companion relationship. Much easier, much calmer, and much more fun!

Examples:

a) Your dog is jumping up on you. You yell "Down!" and flap your hands (this is a great reward for jumping). Dog carries on jumping.

Alternative using your mantra:

Your dog is jumping up on you. You turn away and imagine you can see no dog. Dog ceases jumping and waits for you to come back. Now you can reward him for not jumping!

You are focussing on your dog keeping his feet on the floor

b) Your dog is jumping up on a visitor. You yell "Down!" while your visitor flaps his hands and laughs, saying, "I don't mind" (He does. He really does mind.)

Alternative using your mantra:

You have your dog on a lead before your visitor arrives. You park him (see Key Lead Skill No.2 in Chapter 4 of this book). When he is calm he gets given permission to "Go say Hi", and comes straight back to you for his reward.

You are focussing on your dog greeting calmly

c) Your dog raids the kitchen bin. There is rubbish everywhere. You tell him off, focussing on the mess on the floor. He may think you're just cross and it has nothing to do with him. Or he may think that next time he raids the bin he'll make sure to make himself scarce when you come home. (This is not shame or guilt, just fear.)

Alternative using your mantra:

Your dog raids the kitchen bin. You realise your mistake in leaving him and the bin together unattended. You greet him warmly as usual, clear up the mess without comment and put the bin safely out of his reach. Be sure to leave your dog something he *is* allowed to rip or chew next time you leave him.

You are focussing on your dog's needs, not your own convenience

Focus on what you want, not what you don't want!

What you focus on is what you get.

2. Marker Training

To make sure your dog knows exactly what it is you like, you can mark the split-second she's doing it. You can use your voice - useful as you always have your voice with you. You need to make your marker very short and snappy. "Yes!" is a popular choice. If you say "Good girl" you're likely to spin these words out slowly - "Goooood girrrrrrrl" - so that by the time you've said it your dog is on to something else. You are no longer marking a smart sit, but a shuffle of the paws and a gaze out of the window.

You can also use a clicker. This has the advantage of always sounding the same, so different people can make the exact same marker when they train the dog with it. It doesn't express emotion, so you don't burden your dog with your disappointment or frustration. This can be a plus or a minus. It's nice to be able to inject some enthusiasm into your training with your voice when you need to jizz things up a bit.

You can use either or both. The principle of marking accurately what you like - the moment your dog does it - is the same.

So also is the fact that Marker = Reward. If you mark, with a word or a click, you must now reward your dog. That's the deal you cut with her. If you spoke or clicked by mistake, it doesn't matter - you still reward your dog. You can quickly undo your mistake with a couple of accurate clicks or Yeses.

Once your dog twigs that if she can get you to say Yes, or to click, a reward is guaranteed, you'll suddenly find you have a willing learner who is ready to try things to see what works.

When you want to lead up your dog, for example, instead of chasing her round the kitchen or fighting her off your chest, you can simply stand still holding the lead. Lead = walk = excitement, so your dog will be bouncing around. Now you wait. Wait till she has four feet on the ground, mark with a Yes, and clip the lead on - the going out for a walk is the reward.

You can be imaginative with your rewards! Remember, a reward is something *your dog* finds rewarding, not something you think she ought to like.

But just before we launch into Rewards, I'll mention the No-Reward Marker. This is what you can use to indicate to your dog that she has been unsuccessful and no reward is forthcoming. Please use this very very sparingly or - better still - not at all. You can end up using your words as power steering as you say "Yes. Ah-ah. Nooooooo. Yes. No. Oh no." etc. Your dog is no longer truly making choices, just trying things and seeing whether you respond with a yes (treat) or a No-Reward Marker. It can make your dog very anxious as they really have little idea what it is you want, and can cause them to give up entirely. The only time I may use it is by saying a sad "Oh?" to encourage a re-think.

You can add a Keep Going Signal by way of encouragement. "You've nearly got it - Yes, that's it!" or "Where should you be now? What about your feet? Yes!" I know my dog does not understand the words, but she gets my meaning and tries harder.

It's essential that she's free to try things that don't work, thus finding what does work.

3. Rewards

"Hmm – looks like a training game is coming!"

Let's look at what you need to make sure your dog loves this new choice game!

1. A selection of toys your dog absolutely loves. Balls on ropes; soft tug toys made of fleece, sheepskin, or rabbit skin; and teddy bear-type toys, are all good. Squeaky toys may cause your dog to lose his mind and may not be much use in a training session.

2. Mega-desirable treats! This means treats that your dog will sell her soul for, not dry kibble or pocket fluff. You can get some first-class commercial treats if you hunt carefully, but the best treats tend to be home-prepared, soft, slippery, flavoursome, smelly, and small. Revisit the Rewards section in Chapter 2 of this book, and fill your fridge and your pockets with irresistible goodies. (If you live in a hot country you'll probably want to use a treat-bag, not your pocket!)

If you asked me to run an errand for you, then said, "Here's a lovely bowl of oranges for you as a thank you," I'd be unimpressed. I hate oranges. If you offered me a dry biscuit, that would be so-so, and I may decline it and head away. Now if you were to say "Would you like a piece of chocolate cake?" that would be another matter entirely! I'd be saying, "Is there anything else you'd like me to do?"

So be sure the treats you're offering are worth working for, exactly match your dog's individual preferences, and desirable enough to distract your reactive dog when she's under pressure.

How many rewards should I give?

Don't get hung up over treats: they are a means to an end. You get paid for going to work - why shouldn't your dog? So how many treats should you give? Whatever it takes! I aim to dish out a lot of treats to my crew every day. But they only get a treat when they do something I like. So that means the more things they do that I like, the more treats will come. They get that!

And I don't distinguish between doing and not doing - for instance, stopping barking and not starting barking. Both are rewardable. When my barky dog gets a reward for stopping barking, the others (who may or may not have joined in) get a treat for their silence.

One thing you may find is that kibble or relatively uninteresting treats can work better if you are working on - for example, resting on a mat. Using ultra-exciting treats, speaking excitedly, using a clicker, can all work against you in this situation. So there is a place for lower-value treats - thus saving the heavy artillery for when you're out in the thick of it!

Keep in mind that the ability to take food is a clear signal of your dog's mental state. If she's unable to take treats she normally loves - it's time to make distance! (See Chapter 3 of this book.)

Homework sessions

A word about length of sessions. As suggested above, a lot of your dog's learning will be on-the-go - you'll be catching moments that please you and rewarding them. This may spread into a short practice session for one of the exercises here. But when you have a formal training session, that too should be as short as possible. I aim to work for maybe 60 seconds - and that will include play - or about 10-20 treats. The sessions are very intensive but very short and usually exciting. Nobody has time to get bored!

When you're working outside your sessions will be longer, but only long enough! I'll be showing you how to judge that later on.

4. Pattern Games

This is a name first coined by Leslie McDevitt (see Resources section) for her excellent games designed to help anxious dogs. They are simplicity itself, and their success depends on establishing a quick, light, rhythm. Only one action is required from your dog, and that is marked and rewarded.

Dogs learn by rhythm and patterning (as do we), and these games are a fun way to get what you want very quickly. They can be played anywhere, though it's best to start indoors in a place your dog feels comfortable. For me, that's our small kitchen.

I'm going to give you three pattern games inspired by Leslie McDevitt that will help you to get fast engagement from your dog. Once they know the games well (and they love them), you'll be able to use them as a way to settle your dog in a difficult situation. As long as you are far enough away from his trigger, you can start playing one of these games and get total involvement and joy in the game. The worries your dog had will evaporate as he feels the security and pleasure of playing with you.

Lesson 3: The Focus Game

1. Stand and place a treat on the floor to the right of your foot. Your dog will eat it and possibly sniff about for more. Finding none, she'll look towards you to see if any more treats are coming.

2. Say "YES!" enthusiastically the second she turns to you and place another treat - quickly and with a flourish - to your left.

3. As your dog looks up from eating it, say "YES!" and place another treat to your right, and so on, getting into a fast rhythmic dance.

Once your dog knows the game you'll be able to throw the treat to right or left without having to bend over and place it. It's not a game of "Hunt the Treat," so be sure your dog sees where you drop it so she can grab it instantly and turn. A bowling action is better than a toss as your piece of cheese will land who-knows-where if you toss it.

It may take several short sessions before your dog is keen to run back and forth in front of you like a pendulum. This may take days - don't worry about a timetable. She's learning to focus on you, turning quickly to look at you after grabbing her treat. Repeat the Focus Game till it becomes totally automatic and slick for both of you - and always ends up with smiles from you and that zany expression on your dog's face. Say "All done," and toss her a toy.

Lesson 4: The Name Game

Now we can move forward to the Name Game. Here, we will establish that your dog's name means a fast head-turn.

1. Start with the Focus Game and, once you have a rhythm, add your dog's name *just as she's diving* for the treat. She has time only to grab it and turn.

2. Say "YES!" exactly as her head turns. You are marking the muscle movement in the neck (just like athletes train accuracy).

3. Repeat now till your dog is spinning round, ears flapping, just after you've said her name, and turning with joy and enthusiasm!

4. Stop while you're ahead! About ten treats or a minute or so is enough.

Watchpoint

Be sure you say your dog's name just as she's about to grab the treat then follow with "Yes!" for the head-turn, then toss the treat. The sequence is

(toss treat)
Name
Yes!
Treat
Name
Yes!
Treat ...

Develop a rhythm and make sure these are separate events. Keep your hands together till after you've said Yes, then you can deliver the treat. Don't let all the steps happen at once or confusion will reign!

Lesson 5: The Sit Game

You need to have a firm rhythm established in your Focus Game before embarking on the Sit Game. You're going to break the rhythm in order to move the goalposts, so you have to have a rhythm so that you can break it!

1. Start with your Focus Game until you're both in the groove
2. After a few Yeses and treats, this time when your dog looks at you, *say nothing*
3. She'll likely stare at you and say "I'm looking at you - where's my treat?" Keep waiting
4. She may jump up at you, she may bark at you. Make no response and keep waiting
5. Eventually she will sit. Hurrah! "Yes!" Treat! Toss the treat away from her so she has to get up
6. Repeat from 5 till her sits are quick and fluent.
7. Add the word "Sit" as her bottom is heading for the floor (don't wait till she's sat).

In one short session, or possibly two, your dog has learnt to sit when nothing else is asked of her. You have labelled it as "Sit". And nowhere did you tell your dog to do anything! This is the essence of Choice Training. She worked it out all by herself.

Watchpoint

If you get to step 3 and your dog gets anxious because you're saying nothing, be sure to keep her in the game *without helping her*. So you may smile, relax your stance, you may quietly say, "How are you going to get this treat, then?"

If seconds are passing and your dog is frozen to the spot and getting worried, just go back to the Focus Game for a few treats so she knows she's doing the right thing, then try again. Sooner or later she'll stop worrying and start thinking. This response is not uncommon in a dog who responds to everything with anxiety, or who has always been told what to do in the past. No longer! She's going to learn to stand on her own four feet.

ACTION STEP 21:

Be sure to play these games daily, for just a few treats. Remember training sessions should be very brief and often spontaneous. My dogs know that if I head for the coffee machine there's a good chance of a game or two while coffee is being made. Kettle time is a good time - grab a handful of treats and in the minute it takes your kettle to boil you have done a chunk of training with your dog! While all three games build your dog's confidence, the Name Game is obviously a winner when it comes to building your Stunning Recall (see Resources section).

In this chapter, we have learnt that:

- Choice Training builds your dog's confidence and independence
- It enables your dog to explore his huge capabilities
- Pattern games are very satisfying and a quick way to teach key concepts
- The sky's the limit!

Section 3

Relaxation and Walk Management

Chapter 8
Three essentials for safe walks

1. Impulse Control

This has been mentioned a number of times. Because it's essential! You can't teach a child who is continually trying to do something else because of lack of focus and an attraction to shiny objects (or anything that moves or is edible). The same goes for your dog.

And while the quickest and simplest way to teach your dog this skill is with food, its applications are not limited to food!

Think of:

- your dog calmly waiting for you to open the door till released to go out, then to sit and wait for you while you close the door
- the comfort and safety you'll enjoy doing the same trick with exits from the car
- respect for your furniture
- polite toy play which leaves your fingers intact
- your dog taking treats nicely and still leaving those fingers intact
- no more stealing! no more counter-surfing!
- walking past trees and lamp-posts without your dog hauling you over to check the pee-mail
- being able to pass exciting things without your dog becoming a hooligan

- seeing your dog become more thoughtful and reflective - fewer knee-jerk reactions!
- meeting and greeting politely

The opportunities are endless. All of these lead to a quiet life. When I've boarded individual dogs in my home in the past, I've always found it exhausting to be their impulse control for them. My dogs are not perfect (neither am I!) but life is so easy when you have a responsible dog around, and not a thieving chancer.

For a detailed program to teach your dog impulse control, see the second book in the series **Essential Skills for a Brilliant Family Dog** - *Leave it! How to teach Amazing Impulse Control to your Brilliant Family Dog* (see Resources Section) which you can get free after you get Book 1: *Calm Down!* also free. And if your dog is impetuous and his attention flittered, see the problem-solving e-course listed in the Resources section, which has lots of "recipes" to help you.

ACTION STEP 22:

Teach your dog impulse control. He's not going to learn without being shown. Hey - the book is free! Go get it!

---

2. Emergency Measures: protecting your dog

There are three quick ways to get your dog out of the line of fire when you're out.

Collar Hold

A soft touch on the neck tells Lacy to be still

I've shown you this game in Book 1 and again in Chapter 1 of this book. It's important! Not only are you able to immobilise your dog, and move her behind you as you turn in front of her, but the feel of the back of your hand resting against her neck will be calming to her. Putting your hand in your dog's collar is not a way of grabbing and hauling her about. It's that gentle connection we are always seeking.

Get behind

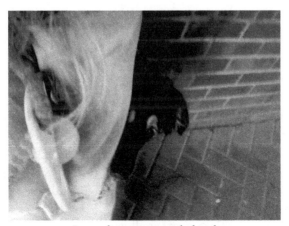

Lacy chooses to get behind

Very useful for giving your dog a hiding place. Teach her to run round you and peep out from behind your legs. One of the advantages of this is that your lead is now going behind your legs, so your dog will not be able to lurch forward. You can partially hide your dog this way, reducing the stimulus to the other dog, or the stranger advancing towards you intent on greeting your fearful dog.

Carwash (aka Middle)

I believe it was Grisha Stewart (Resources section) who chose this moniker! Similar to *Get behind* above, only your dog goes halfway round you and dives between your legs and sits. You can apply gentle pressure by squeezing your legs in - very comforting for some dogs. Carwash is particularly useful for people-fearful dogs. There are few people who will make so bold as to lean forward, advancing their hand towards your crotch, to bend over and touch your dog! Again, the lead is going round the back of your leg, so your dog can't pounce forward at the would-be greeter.

Lacy, if alarmed, may put herself into Carwash. She's telling me she's uncomfortable with the person or people nearby and needs a little reassurance that they won't try to interact with her. Lacy's catchphrase - borrowed from another glamour puss - is "I want to be alone"!

Lacy puts herself in Carwash

Lesson 6 Carwash

1. Have a treat in each hand and your dog facing you
2. Draw her round your right leg with the treat in your right hand
3. As she gets behind you, bring your left hand back to join your right hand between your spread legs and "take over" with that hand, drawing her forward between your legs
4. Encourage your dog to look up to your face, which will produce a sit
5. Repeat so your hand becomes a signal to send her round, with just a treat for sitting.
6. Once she loves this game, and bounces excitedly into position, you can name it "Carwash" (or whatever you like)

ACTION STEP 23:

Get all three of these emergency measures fluent. There's another one to come soon!

3. The muzzle

The first thing to do is to stop seeing the muzzle as a mark of shame.

Many years ago I read of a mother who had written to "Dear Abby" about her little boy who was deaf. She had such feelings of guilt and anxiety about this that she hated his hearing aids - the very thing she should have been glad of! This dislike was rubbing off onto her son, who was getting tricky about wearing them. The advice given was to give the hearing aids the honour and respect and gratitude they warranted. She was to lay out her son's clothes with the hearing aids proudly on the top of the pile. Fitting them to the child at the start of the day was to be an exciting moment of togetherness and hope.

This profound advice made a huge difference to the mother's outlook, and helped her son to cope with being different.

Revise your feelings about muzzles!

The primary purpose of the muzzle, of course, is to prevent anyone getting injured. If your dog has bitten or you feel is likely to bite, then you have a responsibility to protect others (however stupid you may think they are!). You can get muzzles in pretty colours, and even a black one will look cute adorned with ribbons or sparkly star stickers.

The very useful secondary aspect of muzzling your dog, however, is that it keeps people away! Hooray! Just what your anxious dog wants. People will cross the road to avoid this dog who they consider dangerous. Fact is, it's now the safest dog around, because of the muzzle!

You need to stop worrying about what other people think. It's really of little importance. There are other reasons for a dog to be muzzled apart from danger of biting, and keeping people away: maybe your dog eats stones or harvests other unsavoury and dangerous (read: costly vets' bills) things from the environment. Maybe she steals other dogs' toys and then challenges them to a duel. You don't have to apologise for your care and thoughtfulness. And keep in mind that it's worth teaching any dog to be happy with a muzzle. If an awkward or painful procedure is needed at the vet's, it's good if your dog is happy to wear her muzzle and is not subjected to the ignominy of being wrestled into one by strangers.

Be sure to use a basket muzzle, so your dog can pant, drink, bark, and eat treats without difficulty. And don't just buy a muzzle and whap it on her! You'll find a program to acclimatise your dog to the muzzle so that she's keen to put her face into it, in the Resources section.

In this chapter we have learnt that:

- Impulse Control will seep into every corner of your dog's life, and improve it
- You can use three quick fixes to move your dog out of trouble
- Muzzles are not the black beast - they're the white knight in shining armour!

Chapter 9
Relaxation, De-stress, and *Sleep*

The ability to switch off, to relax and restore, is much sought after by people with enormously busy schedules and responsibilities. The most successful build naps and quiet time into their day as a matter of course - and that downtime is inviolable! They have learnt its importance.

Teaching your dog how to switch off is essential to his mental wellbeing. Some dogs don't need to learn this! Cricket the Whippet is happy to spend 22 hours a day under a duvet, reserving her activity for mealtimes and short bursts of awe-inspiring speed. But she has an even temperament and no hang-ups over other dogs or people. Nothing even startles her!

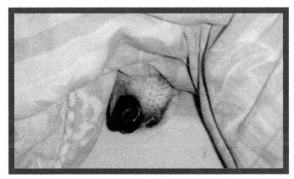

Sky the whippet under the duvet

But it's a sure bet that your reactive and anxious dog will keep pacing and worrying all day unless rest-time is enforced.

Relaxation and sleep

If ever a dog needed its rest and restorative sleep, it's the growly, fearful, or reactive dog. Think how you feel when you're short of sleep and have a challenging day ahead with the family, or at work! You start off on a short fuse, and that may get shorter as the day goes on.

Ensuring your dog gets enough downtime is critically important. It's often at the root of her troubles. Once she's getting enough restorative sleep she'll be better able to cope with all the trials and tribulations of life. As indicated in Book 1, dogs need a massive *17 hours of sleep a day* for optimal stresslessness. Is your dog getting anything like that? If not, you need to help him into a comfortable routine which does not involve endless pacing and activity.

Have a look at Tim, the rescue Border Collie, who I was visiting to work on his dog reactivity outside the house:

While I was there, it became clear that this hyperactive dog was wearing himself out. For the first twenty minutes of my visit he never stopped. He raced in and out of the room, jumped up my front, my back, chewed my hair, poked the other dog, ran off again, paced … never rested.

So I quickly amended my training plan to include some relaxation work straight away. After some active games to get Tim to engage with me, I started teaching him to slow down and relax. After just five minutes of this, his owner expressed amazement at seeing her frantic dog actually lying down still for more than ten seconds at a time!

When I finished the short session and released him, what did he do? Do you think he went straight back into busybusy mode, panting and racing?

Nope. He just slid onto the floor beside us, and as he lay there his head started to loll, his eyelids drooped, and he was … asleep! To the total astonishment of his owner, who had never seen him sleep in the day.

Want to know what I did to achieve this blissful calm state? See the first book in the **Essential Skills for a Brilliant Family Dog** series: *Calm Down! Step-by-Step to a Calm, Relaxed, and Brilliant Family Dog,* free at all e-book stores, to get the exact program. Quite apart from the usefulness of this skill for any dog, anywhere, your reactive dog will hugely benefit. See the Resources section for details.

Watchpoint

Teaching calm and relaxation is *not* teaching a stay exercise (although you will get a solid stay as a result) with the traditional stern shouting and finger-waving. The object is quite different - to change your dog's mental state, not to anchor his physical position.

Learning how to switch off can also help with Separation Anxiety. This is not the place to go through a program for changing this area of distress in your dog, but the Resources section holds some answers for you.

In passing, I'll also mention the Relaxation Protocol (Resources section again). This is a program which takes incremental steps from frantic non-resting dog to chilled-out dog with a lower heart-rate and dreamy feelings of comfort and relaxation. It's a simple program: you don't have to do Day 1 only on Day 1 - repeat each "Day" till you have it right, then move on to the next "Day". It takes time, yes, but it's time well spent helping your dog de-stress. You'll feel as if you've had a relaxation session yourself! It's worth getting started on it to help your dog access the calm side of his mind, which he may have lost sight of in his anxiety.

De-stressing

If you get a fright, your hormones come to your body's rescue and flood the system with what is needed to restore calm. Cortisol provides fuel for fight or flight and is essential to get us out of danger. But if the stressful or frightening stimulus continues or re-occurs, too much cortisol will be circulating, which can lead to longer-term ailments. Imagine if you had a minor car crash. Even though you weren't hurt, your cortisol levels will have shot up. You need a couple of days for them to settle again. Until then you could be very jumpy as soon as you get in a car, or even try to cross the road. It's an unpleasant feeling, and we naturally try to soothe any friend or relative who has had a fright. Rest and tea and nursery food are in order!

Your dog, yet again, is the same! If when walking, he kicks up a fuss at a passing dog, he has just gone through the same experience as you in your car crash. His hormone levels are raised - he's more likely to react to the next dog. Your walk is not now remotely pleasurable! It's exhausting for both of you.

Your dog needs to get home to a safe place and relax and live a boring, uneventful, life for two to three days to allow the levels to go back to normal.

There is no law that dictates that your dog must be walked every day!

He needs exercise, sure, but that can be achieved in a fairly small garden, with some energetic games with a ball or a flirt pole. He needs mental stimulation - yes. But that can be achieved by playing some games involving searching and nosework, tricks, or food-toys.

In general, walks are social outings - essential for young puppies - but they're not exercise. Free running and jumping about till your dog's sides are heaving, his tongue lolling, and his eyes shining, are what you want for exercise.

So, if no-one is enjoying these walks, don't do 'em! You'll be getting tools and techniques from me to transform your dog into a more detached and thoughtful creature. Then you'll be looking for walks with plenty of dogs around to practice your new skills!

Medication

I'll just mention this here briefly, as we looked at meds in more detail in Book 1. I am not (as you know by now) a vet. So you must do your own homework. But there is no shame in getting meds for your dog if that's what he needs in order to lead a normal life. You can start with the herbal-type over-the-counter remedies before upgrading to the class A stuff. These seem to work well with some dogs, and not at all with others, so just try them and see. They also tend to kick in much faster than the prescription drugs. Those that are marketed as fireworks remedies obviously have to start working quickly. You may like to consider visiting a Veterinary Behaviourist before taking this step.

In this chapter we have learnt:

- The importance of rest and sleep for your reactive dog
- The difference between exercise and social walking
- That you don't have to keep up dogwalks if your dog finds them unpleasant
- Meds may help him till his new skills become automatic

Chapter 10
Distance revisited

We took a look at the sophisticated language dogs use to converse in Book 1. We're going to take another look at it here from a different angle: how to use your knowledge of this to your advantage on walks. And it's appearing as another new Action Step, just in case Action Step 9 in Book 1 slipped past you ...

ACTION STEP 24:

This step is critical! *Show your dog she never has to meet another dog or person ever again.* When you and your dog see something coming that you know will upset her, you say a cheery "Let's go!", turn, and head in another direction. Your reward will be the relief you see in her face.

This is one of the most important moments for you to capture - the moment your dog sees another dog, causing a transformation in her whole body posture. She can go from relaxed and curvy to stiff and tense in the blink of an eye. Your eye, that is! If she's worried she may well be unable to give the calming signal of a soft blink or a lookaway. So you help her. Keeping your hands soft and your shoulders relaxed, you make a happy distracting noise and head off purposefully - elsewhere.

You've learnt that walking straight towards another dog is very poor form and can be misconstrued as aggressive. So why would you do this? Answer: because man has made lovely straight footpaths, roads, and pavements for us all to walk along! Left to their own devices, dogs will greet in a nonchalant, curvy, fashion. The size of the curve and the distance from each other depends on a number of factors, which may include relative size, age, sex, and manner.

So without climbing a tree or scrambling over a wall into someone's garden, our only choice to avoid advancing straight towards another dog is to turn and go. This is not a dramatic, screaming, exit! It's a gentle curve away - as softly as you can manage.

Note that many of our pavements and footpaths are more like tunnels! There may be hedges, walls, and fences down one side; there may be parked cars down the other. Being in a tunnel makes the fight or flight response kick in much faster. Imagine walking down a narrow alleyway one dark night and you see a suspicious character lurking halfway along. You are definitely going to feel trapped, and maybe start panicking. This is how your dog feels!

Remember that a dog's personal space requirement is way bigger than ours.

The fourth emergency measure!

This is your "get out of jail" card promised in Chapter 8 of this book. This will be invaluable to you to remove your dog instantly from a situation she may not even be aware of. Whereas in Action Step 24 above, you need your dog to be aware of the oncoming hazard so she can appreciate your speedy response in getting her out of trouble, in this Key Lead Skill you can act before she's even seen it. Invaluable for when a dog suddenly appears from nowhere just a few yards ahead!

Key Lead Skill no. 6
Emergency Turn "Happy"

1. You are walking with your dog on lead beside you
2. You see an imaginary hazard up ahead
3. Stop (your dog will feel this on the lead) as you call out "Happy!"
4. Your dog will turn to see what's going on
5. Back up, smiling and connecting with your dog as she comes towards you, and you run backwards
6. When you have her full attention, turn and head away briskly with her beside you
7. Finish the sequence with a treat as you walk away from the hazard

Play this game frequently. Your dog should get to love this and be very quick: "Ha, you can't catch me out!" Nine times out of ten play it as a game - only occasionally will you use it for real. Be sure to go back to playing it as a game once you've used it in earnest: you don't want your dog thinking that "Happy!" means "Danger! Dog incoming!" As a nice spin-off, you'll find her paying more attention to you as you walk - just in case you start this game!

Why that loopy word "Happy!"? It's very hard to say "Happy!" while looking worried or sounding angry. When your dog turns to look at you, isn't it better that she sees her lovely owner looking happy? You also have to consider the person with the dog coming towards you. If you yell the dog's name, they may react by trying to haul their dog away from this mad person with their dangerous dog and set up a chain of events you want to avoid! And if your dog's name is Chappie, or Mattie, or something that sounds too like Happy, try "Smiley!". Of course you can use any word or sound you want, but using a word that will influence the outcome is handy. I am indebted to one of my students - Janet, with her Leonberger Chloe - who came up with this ingenious and effective word.

ACTION STEP 25:

Learn the Emergency Turn inside out, till you can initiate it at a second's notice. If you practice it daily, not only will your dog get very quick at it, but you will have it honed and ready for when you need it, without first panicking, clutching the lead and wondering what to do!

In this chapter we've learnt that:

- Distance is our friend
- You always need to keep an eye on your distance
- If that distance shrinks too much, you can get away swiftly and painlessly
- We are Happy!

Chapter 11
Managing walks

Equipment

In Chapter 1 of this book we looked at equipment in detail. In addition to the right gear, you now have six Key Lead Skills to help you. As you are by now getting used to your dog's new kit, you will also - as a team - be getting very fluent at those lead skills.

Consider these skills a priority. Gentle handling is key to making your walks pleasant and uneventful. Think of the ace showjumper: his hands are soft, his use of the reins sympathetic. If he keeps sawing at his horse's mouth, the animal will get a "hard mouth" and become unresponsive to a light touch on the reins. In the same way, your dog can get a "hard neck" from all the lead-jabbing that has been going on, and you have to hoist him into the middle of next week for him to notice a touch on the lead.

Working together with your dog, your gentle pressure on the lead being echoed by his gentle pressure in return, will help to bring you the results you want.

ACTION STEP 26:

Re-visit Chapter 1 of this book and ensure you have ditched any aversive gear and replaced it with effective, friendly, safe, and helpful, equipment that you are both enjoying using.

A word about car reactivity

Sometimes, just getting to your walking place is fraught with hazards! Your dog barks at everything he sees on the car journey, be it dog, horse, person, child, bike ... So by the time you arrive, your dog is already in a highly aroused state, twitchy and ready to bark at the next thing he sees.

So consider what you can do to make your car rides more peaceful - not to mention safer. A dog leaping about in the car barking is not helping your concentration on the road!

What will usually make a huge difference is restricting your dog's vision. If he can't see it, he can't bark at it. Obviously he needs to be restrained in one area of the car for his safety - not to mention everyone else's. A loose dog in a car is deemed an "unsecured load" and is certainly against the law in the UK, and I suspect elsewhere as well. In an emergency stop, 50 lbs of dog hitting the back of your seat at 40 miles an hour is not going to do either of you any good. Personally, I favour robust, non-rattling, crates - which must have an escape door to the inside of the car in case of accident. I'm not convinced about the efficacy of dog seatbelt restraints and I'd never leave a dog tied up in the car unsupervised anyway - that's an accident waiting to happen, as he jumps off the seat getting his leg caught in the handbrake lever ...

So now there are three possibilities:

1. Cover the crate. With a dark cloth, cover the crate so that your dog can't see out of the window. Leave plenty of space for air circulation lower in the crate.

2. Cover the windows near your dog's place in the car. You could do all the back windows - you can't, of course cover the front windows! But a curtain dividing front from back may work for you. A quick and easy way to cover the windows is to use black-out material or strongly-patterned fabric. Choose one that doesn't fray and you won't even need to hem it. To fix the panels over the windows, you can use either velcro dots (put the fuzzy side on the car and the spiky side on the fabric), or hem in tiny magnets which will attach themselves readily to the metal of the car window frame. You can throw these up very quickly, then rip them down just as quickly when you are carrying hoomins*.

    *LOLspeak for people, in case you're not familiar with the term!

3. Another option that works well with some dogs is a Calming Cap - a kind of soft mask you fit over your dog's face which makes the world appear fuzzy and unresolved. Naturally you'd acclimatise your dog to this first, using the same method you'll see to teach a dog to love his muzzle (in the Resources section). Remember we want our dog to be less stressed, not more stressed, so for some dogs this may be a no-no.

Those Key Lead Skills

ACTION STEP 27:

Get the Key Lead Skills you found in Chapters 4 and 10 of this book fluent and easy. If you have poor motor skills or you just struggle with left and right, practice with a friend. Children will be happy to volunteer to "be a dog" for you! Once these skills are a firm habit, walks will be so much easier!

So use a long line where appropriate, keep your hands soft, and keep your distance! You'll need to be very familiar with all these skills before embarking on the techniques coming up.

Muzzle

We've frequently visited muzzles so far in this book - in Chapter 1, Chapter 3, Action Step 18, and Chapter 8.

The key points are that a muzzle

- keeps people away
- helps you relax

If you feel more relaxed knowing for certain your biting dog cannot bite anything, go for it!

ACTION STEP 28:

Shed your pre-conceptions. Do what is right for your dog.

Incoming dog!

This is the bane of many a dog-owner's existence! The loose, rampaging dog. Hearing the owner in the distance calling out "It's ok, he's friendly," is no help whatever. And perhaps the dog is ownerless, or virtually ownerless, as his owner slopes off, shoulders hunched, talking on the phone, no interest in his dog who, in any case, has zero recall. The owner knows this and isn't about to demonstrate his miserable training failure to you! So asking the person to call their dog is more often than not fruitless.

What can you do? Here are a number of things you can try. Nothing is guaranteed to work, but in my experience using one or more of these tactics you can usually escape unscathed. Remember the other dog is not to blame for his unruly behaviour: it's not his fault he has no training. So treat him with the same kindness you'd want for your own dog.

- First thing, as ever, is distance. Turn on your heel, using Key Lead Skills 5 and/or 6, and march smartly away, chatting to your dog

- And the other first thing is to relax your hands on the lead! Nothing transmits fear as quickly as the lead being yanked and your dog half-strangled

- Collar hold (see Chapter 1 of this book). I call my reactive dog over to me as I see an incoming dog and slip my hand in her loose collar, the back of my hand lying against her neck. She relaxes and waits beside me. If we're so calm that we're utterly boring, the other dog often gives up and heads off. (But if required Lacy can give a magnificent withering stare which will intimidate many dogs!)

- "The House is on Fire!": Emergency Recall x 10. Yell excitedly at your dog while you turn and race away fast. The surprise element can often work

- If you have a companion, teach them to call out "Incoming!" as soon as they see something heading your way, giving you time to decide on your exit strategy

- If your dog is genuinely ok off-lead (are you absolutely sure?) and incomer doesn't look dangerous, drop the lead while you keep away. Don't interfere. This may surprise you!

- Some people have success tossing a handful of treats at the dog as he arrives. I wouldn't do that if the dog looked ferocious and may misinterpret my arm action!

- If you have a walking stick or staff, swing it *gently* back and forth like a pendulum in front of you and your dog. This is *odd* and may cause the incomer to back off. You're not trying to hit the dog!

- No staff? Try twirling your lead round in a big circle, like a windmill. Ensure any metal bits are in your hand. You don't, of course, want to hurt the dog, and you certainly don't want to whack your ankle with a lead clasp. Again, a slow circle is odd enough to get most nosy dogs away. Practice this first

- A pop-up umbrella - the type where you press a button and it opens - can be very handy, especially if you have a small dog. Ping it open in front of your dog. This will at the very least give pause to the rushing incomer. If it's a sighthound racing in intent on your small fluffy this may well be a lifesaver

- With the swinging staff, the windmill lead, and the umbrella, teach your own dog at home first, and associate this new game of yours with treats and good things

- Small dog: you may be tempted to pick him up. This could work, but equally it could cause the incomer (who was only nosy) to grab this fluffy toy as you swing it up in the air. Then your arm may get bitten too. You grabbing your dog can also make your dog more afraid - and as you bend, your face will be at incoming dog tooth level: not good. So teach your little dog to jump into your arms instead.

- Gadgets like air horns and aversive sprays: *wah-wah*. This is blanket bombing that will affect your dog as well as the incomer, making him more frightened than ever. Skip them.

- Ignore the abuse you will quite possibly get from the other owner. I have been accused of kicking or hitting their dog (never), of enticing their dog away on purpose (?!), and of being unable to control my (leashed) dog while their (loose) dog snapped at his face. They know they're in the wrong, and they try to cover their confusion and embarrassment by going on the offensive. And it can sure be offensive sometimes as the air turns blue! The abusers have always been male. Just sayin'.

ACTION STEP 29:

Practice any of these suggestions you like the look of when there is no threat. Make it a fun game for your dog, so she's a willing partner.

Loose Lead Walking

How on earth can teaching my dog to walk nicely on the lead beside me help with managing her reactivity on walks? Easy!

- It gives her a position she is secure in, and where she can look up and see your face
- It's a party trick she can depend upon to produce rewards
- It gives her a focus - something to be doing other than scanning the horizon for approaching hazards
- It puts you into a companionable bubble with your dog as you walk through the world together

ACTION STEP 30:

For a complete program on achieving this, go to the third book in the series **Essential Skills for a Brilliant Family Dog:** *Let's Go! Enjoy Companionable Walks with your Brilliant Family Dog* (for where to find this step-by-step book, check the Resources section).

Wide open spaces

Choose your area carefully! There are cultural differences about off-lead walking, so you need to know what the position is in your neck of the woods. Here in the UK we enjoy freedom with our dogs on the vast network of public footpaths and bridle paths hallowed by history, nationally-owned forests, many beaches, Areas of Outstanding Natural Beauty, national parks, and - of course, farmers' fields with permission.

This may not be an option in some countries - but there has to be somewhere you can take your dog and enjoy free running. As this is an essential freedom for your pet - enshrined in law in the UK and I'm sure many other enlightened countries - perhaps it's time for you to do a bit of civil agitating and ensure proper facilities for dogs to enjoy full physical and mental health.

Having the right to this freedom does not absolve you of responsibility for your dog! But having a wide open space where you can see a long way will make minding your dog miles easier. You have early warning of anything untoward, and your dog can enjoy watching other people and dogs at a distance, maybe hundreds of yards, without fear.

If your dog is a maniac for his toy - so much the better. Always provided he's not guardy over it, of course. If you can't presently guarantee distraction by offering to toss a ball or frisbee, this is a skill you want to develop!

As always on walks, avoid tunnels - narrow alleyways of buildings or hedgerows, narrow streets with tunnels of garden walls and parked cars, narrow footpaths.

Where are we going with this?

So far I have given you lots of background to what your dog is about (Book 1) and lots of tricks and techniques for you to learn (Book 2). It may have surprised you that I go into such detail with things that may not at first appear to be directly linked to your problems. But you don't start your child on trigonometry and calculus! You start with moving counters around and exploring concepts of bigger and smaller. So you need to look at why your dog does what he does first. There's nothing I've given you in these two books that I feel could be omitted. It's a holistic approach to understanding and treating reactivity.

In Book 3 we'll be getting down to the nitty-gritty and exploring methods that have been proven to work to lower stress, anxiety, fear, and frustration, in your dog. These methods will, of course, all be force-free. There is no place for force, intimidation, or coercion in a loving relationship.

Just as a trailer - a cliffhanger for you! - these are broadly the areas you can look forward to covering:

Counter-conditioning and De-sensitisation

Control Unleashed (Leslie McDevitt) - specifically "Look at That"

BAT (Behavior Adjustment Training - Grisha Stewart) in all its glory

By all means purchase the relevant books (see Resources section) if you want to go into great detail with them. They are excellent. But if you're like me, you don't want to buy a car manual and get under the bonnet with a spanner!

You'd rather a mechanic translated it for you into what you need to know and can relate to. I'm going to make it all very accessible and give you what you need to have success, step by step, just as I give it to my students in person.

> "Thanks very much for your time and help. I was really glad to see how well Dexter responded today. It has given me the confidence to help him. Dex and I will enjoy our exercises and getting to know one another."
> *Debbie and Dexter, Border Collie, anxious, over-wrought*

> "Sam's doing really well - he's much happier all round which is fab."
> *Ashleigh and Sam, Border Collie rescue, super fearful of everything, at home and out*

> "Both dogs are doing really well, Coco is so much better going out for a walk and Rocky has calmed down. Thank you so much for all your help."
> *Sharon with Coco and Rocky, Jack Russell Terriers, highly reactive and noisy!*

In this chapter we have learnt:

- More about walk management, including escapes and incoming dogs
- How to minimise car reactivity
- The importance of the Action Steps from the earlier chapters
- There is exciting stuff coming!

Conclusion

We've travelled a long way on our journey into the whys and wherefores and the what-can-you-do-about-its of your reactive and anxious dog. We've covered:

- What equipment you should have or shun
- The anatomy of rewards and rewarding
- Building confidence - for you and your dog
- Critical lead skills
- Choice training plus a bit of science if you want it
- How to manage walks, distance, and escape
- Relaxation

You are well on the way to enjoying a far calmer relationship with your dog. The future does not look so grim. Now you not only understand more about why what's happening is happening, but you have techniques and strategies to change things!

You should be noticing big changes already.

Maybe you're wondering when we're going to get down to brass tacks and learn more techniques to help you - wonder no longer! In the next book we'll be going into detail to help you achieve your goals of having a calm and "normal" dog (what's normal anyway?), a dog you can rely on, a dog you can easily manage, and a dog you can enjoy.

Resources

For a very thorough, in-depth, approach, where I will be on hand to answer all your questions, go to

brilliantfamilydog.teachable.com

where you'll find info about the online course which takes all this to the next level, giving you personal support and encouragement as well as all the lessons and techniques you need to change your life with your Growly Dog.

For a free taster course: **www.brilliantfamilydog.com/growly**

And for loads of articles on Growly Dogs and Choice Training, go to **www.brilliantfamilydog.com** where you'll also find a course on solving everyday dog and puppy problems.

You'll also find the **Essential Skills for a Brilliant Family Dog** series of e-books helpful. Take a holistic view of your relationship with your dog and work on new skills inside the house as well as when you're out. If your dog has always had to be kept on lead because you were afraid he was not safe, you'll definitely need Book 4 for your new life!

Book 1 Calm Down! *Step-by-Step to a Calm, Relaxed, and Brilliant Family Dog*
Book 2 Leave it! *How to teach Amazing Impulse Control to your Brilliant Family Dog*
Book 3 Let's Go! *Enjoy Companionable Walks with your Brilliant Family Dog*

Book 4 Here Boy! *Step-by-step to a Stunning Recall from your Brilliant Family Dog*

And you'll be pleased to know that Book 1 is currently free at all e-book stores!

Here are the links to all the resources mentioned in this book:

Books by other authors:

I'll Be Home Soon: How to Prevent and Treat Separation Anxiety by Patricia McConnell, pub First Stone, 2010

Control Unleashed: Creating a Focused and Confident Dog by Leslie McDevitt, pub Clean Run Productions LLC, 2007 http://controlunleashed.net/book.html

Behavior Adjustment Training 2.0: New Practical Techniques for Fear, Frustration, and Aggression in Dogs by Grisha Stewart, pub Dogwise Publishing, 2016

Dog Tricks: Fun and Games for Your Clever Canine by Mary Ray and Justine Harding, pub Hamlyn 2005

Brain Games for Dogs: Fun ways to build a strong bond with your dog and provide it with vital mental stimulation by Claire Arrowsmith, pub Firefly Books, 2010

101 Dog Tricks: Step by Step Activities to Engage, Challenge, and Bond with Your Dog by Kyra Sundance, Quarry Books, 2007

Websites:
www.muzzleupproject.com - all things muzzle
www.goodfordogs.co.uk/products - Wiggles Wags and Whiskers Freedom Harness - UK and Europe [This is me. If you buy from me I will benefit financially, but it won't cost you any more.]

http://2houndswholesale.com/Where-to-Buy.html - Wiggles Wags and Whiskers Freedom Harness - rest of the world

https://www.youtube.com/watch?v=1OHEB41yRdU - one of many calming sound recordings

https://positively.com/dog-wellness/dog-enrichment/music-for-dogs/canine-noise-phobia-series/ - for desensitisation

http://en.turid-rugaas.no/calming-signals---the-art-of-survival.html - dog body language

http://championofmyheart.com/relaxation-protocol-mp3-files/ audio files for the Relaxation Protocol

http://www.thundershirt.com - for Thundershirt and Calming Cap

https://www.youtube.com/watch?v=Mtn-BeI9lHE - *Pattern Games: Clicking for Confidence and Connection* by Leslie McDevitt, dvd 2011, Tawzer Dog LLC

https://www.youtube.com/watch?v=UGcyier95sw - watch dogs drive cars and fly planes! Really!

http://www.thekennelclub.org.uk/kcdog - KC Dog: section of the UK Kennel Club devoted to protecting dogs' rights

Force-free training hubs:
http://www.apdt.co.uk/dog-owners/local-dog-trainers - UK resource for force-free trainers

http://www.petprofessionalguild.com/PetGuildMembers - global resource for force-free trainers

http://grishastewart.com/cbati-directory/ - global resource for specialist Certified BAT Instructors

Alternative practitioner societies:
www.ttouch.com
www.ttouchteam.co.uk
www.k9-massageguild.co.uk
www.massageawareness.com
www.caninebowentechnique.com

Works consulted for Chapter 6:

http://www.britannica.com/biography/Sigmund-Freud accessed 2016

Mischel, W., et al. (1989). *Delay of gratification in children.* Science, 24 4 (4907), 933–938
https://www.apa.org/helpcenter/willpower-gratification.pdf accessed 2016

Casey, B. J., et al. (2011). *Behavioral and neural correlates of delay of gratification 40 years later.* Proceedings of the National Academy of Sciences, 10 8 (36), 14998–15003
http://www.nobelprize.org/nobel_prizes/medicine/laureates/1904/pavlov-bio.html accessed 2016

http://psychology.about.com/od/classicalconditioning/a/pavlovs-dogs.htm accessed 2016

Skinner, B.F. (1938) *The Behavior of Organisms: An Experimental Analysis,* New York; Appleton-Century

Skinner, B.F. (1951) *"How to teach animals"* Scientific American

Reynolds, G.S. (1968), *A Primer of Operant Conditioning.* Palo Alto, California: Scott, Foresman

Bailey, B, and M.B. Bailey (1996) *Patient Like the Chipmunks.* Eclectic Science Productions

http://www.clickertraining.com/karen accessed 2016

Mary R. Burch and Jon S. Bailey (1999), *How Dogs Learn,* Wiley, NY

Essential Skills for your *Growly* but
Brilliant Family Dog

Book 3

Calm walks with your Growly Dog

Strategies and techniques for your fearful,
aggressive, or reactive dog

Beverley Courtney

Introduction

We've looked at WHY your dog is doing what she does.

We've looked at WHAT you can do to start to make big changes.

Now we're going to see HOW to put those changes into action.

No longer are you the owner of "that nasty dog" who is the curse of the neighbourhood. No longer do you have to walk at the *Hour of the Difficult Dog* in order to avoid every living creature on the planet.

This is where I'm going to give you specific techniques to deal with your dog's reactivity - on the ground. Together we will change your walks to pleasant outings, your time on the road will be less stressful for both of you - you'll know just how to keep your dog calm and happy. And when *he's* calm and happy, *you're* calm and happy!

Along with the skills you've already learnt, you will know exactly what to do in any given situation, because you'll know why it's happening, what you'd like to happen - and how to achieve that.

> "I have had a brilliant walk with him today and he was really good with cars, people and other dogs with limited reactions. He seems to enjoy meeting other people and dogs now." Joan and Shep, Border Collie

Can you believe that in a few short weeks this could be you?

Why can I help you?

I, too, am one of those people with a dog who is wonderful at home - but outside was another story. Lacy's hackles would stand up like spines on a porcupine. She'd lunge and plunge, choking on her collar. She'd look for all the world as if she wanted to tear the other dog - and person - limb from limb. For all the dogs I've lived with, I'd never had this problem before.

What made this all so much worse was that I am a professional dog trainer! Someone who helps people get the best from their dog! Clearly I had a huge gap in my learning, and it was urgent that I plugged that gap as soon as possible. I needed to help my dog, and it was clear that there are plenty of other people out there wrestling with this largely misunderstood problem.

So I embarked on further studies. I devoured everything I could find which promoted a force-free approach to the problem. I already knew that the best way to interact with any animal (or person, for that matter) is by encouraging and rewarding the response you want, rather than demanding, commanding, and manipulating. I learnt why my dog was doing what she does, so I could reject anything that made life worse for her, or which debased my own humanity.

I could say my studies culminated with becoming a Certified Behavior Adjustment Training Instructor (CBATI), but that simply marked a stage in my learning. Every dog I work with has an individual history, an individual personality, and an individual owner. There's no one-size-fits-all. My learning deepens with each new dog.

Listening to these dogs' owners and studying the dogs themselves leads me to a bespoke training program for each one. And once you've read through these books you'll be able to choose what will work for you, and your dog - in your life.

Take care, though, if you are selecting strategies, not to throw the baby out with the bathwater! Try everything I offer you before making any decisions about what will or will not work in your case.

Where do I begin?

These three books stand alone, but are best consumed together, in order.

- The first tells you what's going on and why - and some of this may surprise you. It's essential to understand a problem before attempting to fix it. This book should bring you lots of "Aha!" moments.

- The second book goes into the detail of what you're going to change and how, what approaches will work best, and what you need to make it all work. Lots of Lessons in this section. And much of this will involve change for *you*: exciting!

- And the third book gets you out there with your dog, enjoying a new way of walking and interacting with her, and making the episodes you used to experience - mercifully! - a thing of the past. Lots of Lessons here, and Troubleshooting sections to cover all the "what ifs" you'll come up with.

My suggestion is to read through each book first, then while your brain is filtering and processing this information, you can go back to the start and work through the Action Steps and Lessons with your dog.

For ease of reading, your dog is going to be a he or a she as the whim takes me. He and she will learn the exact same way and have similar responses. There will be just a few occasions when we're discussing only a male or a female, and that will be clear.

So, if you haven't already done so, I suggest you read Books 1 and 2 before embarking on Book 3. (And there's a special offer for you on Book 1! Who doesn't love a special offer?) This way you'll be up to speed with what I'm talking about, you'll get much more out of the material, and you'll be able to put it into action straight away!

Don't waste another minute before starting to help your dog make the change.

Section 1

Desensitisation and Counterconditioning

Chapter 1
What does it mean?

Desensitisation and Counterconditioning (let's call them DS and CC) form a common and effective method for reducing fear (DS) and replacing it with something better (CC). It can be a long, slow, business. But if your dog is already used to the language of doing something in order to earn a reward, it will be quicker. The Precious Name Game (Lesson 1 in Book 1, and Action Step 21 in Book 2) is an example of this.

Desensitisation

Desensitisation works on the emotional response your dog is having. Typically the dog is exposed to the thing she's afraid of at a distance or level (if a sound) at which she can remain calm. The ability to take treats is a fair indicator of your dog being ok. (Could you eat a piece of cake while a mad axe-man was running towards you?) Only gradually is the distance closed, or the level increased, as the dog demonstrates that she's ok with that. It must be done gradually, maybe one yard of the 100 yards' distance closed in one session.

You could spend some time on this before your dog is able to stay calm when the thing that worries her is closer or louder. DS will bring you to a level of acceptance, but no further. Desensitisation is at the heart of Puppy Socialisation, Habituation, and Familiarisation.

Imagine you're afraid of spiders. (If you really are, perhaps you'd prefer to substitute mice or something else that won't upset you in these examples.) You are terrified of them, panic on sight of them, hyperventilate, look for an escape route, and so on. Would putting you in a room full of spiders help?

I don't think so. This system is called flooding and is largely discredited - certainly for working with dogs. It may appear to reduce the reaction, but this could be because your dog has slipped into a state of "learned helplessness". He is a victim - nothing he does will change the situation, so he shuts down and suffers it. This, by the way, is why people often tell me their dog is "fine!" when he is far from fine.

You may be ok if we're in a large hall and I tell you there is a spider in a glass case at the other end of the hall. If you can cope with that without any of your usual symptoms, we may be able to walk down the hall a few steps while you remain calm. If we continue, at some stage you'll panic and want to leave. Only very gradually would we raise the intensity of the object of your fear. Eventually you would be able to be in a room with a spider on the wall - without panicking. You may not be overjoyed about the presence of the spider, but repeated exposure has shown you that you don't have to actively be afraid.

The origin of the fear, by the way, is not important. You may be afraid of spiders because one fell on your face, or because your mother shooed them away with a broom whenever she saw them. The only fears we're born with are the fear of loud noises, and fear of falling. Everything else is a learned fear. And your dog could have learned to fear something by association with a totally different experience - a firework went off as he first looked at a child on a bike, for instance. Any child on a bike is now "dangerous". The joy of DS/CC is that it can be used for fears, anxiety, phobias (irrational fears), as well as aggression - whether motivated by the chase instinct or wishing to scare the thing away. It works on the emotions.

Coco poodle learns to watch animals on tv – calmly

Counterconditioning

This is where Counterconditioning comes in. Once the fear reaction is diminished, we can start replacing that sinking feeling with something better. The easiest way with dogs is to use treats to change their response. So the association with the thing they feared changes from "scary thing = panic" to "scary thing = food". If your dog turns to you for a treat when he sees something hitherto frightening, then he can't be staring at it and barking.

Back to spiders: every time you point out a spider to me, or even mention a spider, I give you a reward (money, a token, a star on a chart, slice of chocolate cake - whatever works for you). Gradually your fear of spiders has changed through tolerance, to actually associating spiders with good outcomes. The fear response has died out and been replaced with a warmer feeling about the beasties.

A simple illustration for a dog who reacts to cyclists could be:

- Start a great distance away from a cyclist who is not coming towards you.
- Gradually close that gap (gradually may mean weeks) till you can see and hear the cyclist clearly.
- Start a great distance away from multiple cyclists - perhaps on a hill looking down on a cycling event.
- Gradually get nearer to the cyclists.
- If a cyclist comes towards you, turn and get away.
- If your dog shows her fear response, turn and get away - you got just too close.
- Eventually you'll reach a stage where your dog can see and hear cyclists (not coming nearer) without reacting.

That's all Desensitisation.

This is where the Counter-conditioning kicks in.

- You start to reward your dog for being near the cyclists.
- Gradually let a cyclist head towards you for a while, till you've given your treats, then you move off (two rewards here - one is food, the other distance).
- At some stage your dog will start to point out cyclists to you in order to get a treat. (Don't ask a cyclist to feed your dog - this is too confrontational.)

If a fully-armed soldier jumped out of a doorway in front of you on the street, you'd probably have a shock - and a pretty big fear reaction! Unless ... you live on an army base, or in a war zone. You'd be so used to soldiers everywhere that you wouldn't bat an eyelid.

This is a system that will usually work over time. But there are much quicker and more effective ways - ways that involve the dog in making the decisions, giving her control over her own actions and responses. I'll be showing you these in the next two sections.

In the next chapter we'll take a look at other things you can affect with DS/CC.

In this chapter we've seen that:

- Slow and steady wins the race
- We can change our dog's perception of scary things
- We are working on the dog's emotions

Chapter 2
Extra sensitivities

Touch sensitivity

This little girl is about to stop petting

Some dogs, especially but not confined to, rescue dogs, are very touch sensitive. They startle when touched, they may growl or more. This could be a learned response in order to keep them safe on the street; it could be as a result of ill-treatment; it could be a symptom of illness (get that vet check!). Some people complain that their dog asks for petting, then after a while turns on the petter and growls or snaps.

A good method for relieving pressure with a dog who is sensitive to touch is to use this method, popularised by Grisha Stewart.

Lesson 7: The Five Second Rule

1. Your dog approaches and solicits affection
2. Touch or stroke her gently for five seconds
3. Disconnect, remove your hands, stare into space
4. Your dog will either poke your hands for more petting, saying, "Don't stop - I was enjoying that!" or move away, perhaps with a shake-off (to settle the hairs back down) muttering, "Thank goodness they stopped. I've had enough." You'll be familiar with this response if you've ever looked after small children, who will push you away when they've had enough comforting.
5. If he wants more attention when you stop, you can do another five seconds.
6. If your dog is super-touch-sensitive, make it three seconds. Known visitors and known children, three seconds. Unknown people, zero seconds.

This is a system you should use with your young puppy - and it's especially important that your children learn to respect their puppy's feelings. No nightmare photos on the internet please, of a child smothering a very anxious-looking dog.

Along with the Five Second Rule, make sure your touch-sensitive dog is ok with the Collar Hold (see Book 1, and again in Book 2). Be sure the collar is as loose as it safely can be, and be sure you're not pulling on the collar, only sliding your hand in.

Sound sensitivity

Many reactive or fearful dogs are also sound sensitive. Fireworks; sudden bangs and crashes from building works; high-pitched sounds from electric motors that we can't hear (think fridge, vacuum cleaner). Border Collies, with their superb hearing, are amongst those most often affected - but any dog can react to pain in the ears. You can get your dog used to these sounds by playing sound recordings to them from an early age (conscientious breeders will be doing this with their puppies from 2-3 weeks old). See the Resources section for what to use.

The trick is to start playing the sounds so quietly that you can barely hear them, while a pleasant activity is going on - keeping you company around the house; lying close to you; chewing a bone - for instance. Gradually increase the volume till the bangs and screeches are pretty sharp but not eliciting a response. Any time you get the slightest whiff of a fear response, go back a few steps.

Dogs have been proven to find Mozart (and any classical music from the 18th and early 19th centuries) relaxing - it's to do with the rhythm and tempo. And there are music video channels on the internet devoted to relaxing sounds for dogs. I have not experienced tv for dogs, but I understand its calming programmes work on similar principles.

Fear of loud noises, as we have seen, is a fear we are born with. Many dogs will startle at a loud noise (normal), but some will descend into a pitiful state of anxiety and distress, from pacing - down to quivering and drooling. This could be because their experience tells them that one bang will be followed by many more bangs and whistles (think Fireworks displays). Or it could be that they are more sound sensitive than usual. This is commonly found in reactive dogs.

My sound-sensitive Border Collie Tip would disappear at the first "Wheeeee!" of a rocket going up. She knew that bangs would follow so she'd burrow under a table or chair to hide from the noise. So her reaction was to a fairly subdued but distinct noise which she knew was a precursor of big noises.

233

You can help your dog in the event of fireworks bangs and crashes, by making a den and covering it with a cloth. Draw your curtains, shut the doors, turn up the tv or specific dog-relaxing recording, and relax yourself. There's no harm in gently soothing your frightened dog, but you won't be able to "comfort" her out of it. There are also calming devices (see Resources section) and calming touches you can use. For difficult cases, consider some over-the-counter remedies for fireworks (see Book 2). For extreme cases where the dog is damaging property and herself in her efforts to escape the barrage, you may need something more powerful from the vet.

We get few thunderstorms in the UK, but in some parts of the world they are so frequent that a DS/CC program would be essential from the start - with the breeder in the litter.

ACTION STEP 31

Practice Desensitisation and Counterconditioning, starting with anything that you can control which your dog finds just slightly worrying. Don't wait for a thunderstorm, where you have no control, and which may be your dog's vision of hell. If he gives forth a cascade of fear and alarm barking at a knock on the front door, you could start by desensitising knocks on tables and internal doors, for example.

In this chapter we've seen that:

- Puppies need a structured program of DS/CC to touch and sound
- We get used to things in the same way as your dog does
- "Familiarity breeds contempt"

Section 2

Look at That

Chapter 3
What is it?

Amber needs to study what she's seeing

Look at That has quite rightly entered the dog training canon as a must-have skill. It originated with Leslie McDevitt in her excellent *Control Unleashed* series of books and videos (see Resources section).

Leslie is passionate about honouring the dog. In the same way that you accept your child as an individual "warts and all", you accept your dog - just as he is. He has an opinion on life, and it's up to the sensitive owner to find that out and respect his thoughts and ideas.

I have four very different personalities in my dogs. There is room in life to give them what they need. Right at this moment while I work, for instance, one is outside dozing on the grass and keeping half an eye on the chickens, one is curled up in a small bed near me, another is stretched out on a large bed just behind me, and the fourth is upstairs in my bed under the duvet. It's not for me to dictate where and how they feel comfortable.

This approach is a huge step forward in dog training. It came at a time when reward-based training was becoming generally accepted - but many people had grasped the method without the reasoning, and were replacing their old "command" mentality (you'll do it because I say so) with a "bribing" method (you'll get this treat if you do it). While that was a great improvement on the punishment-based training commonly used up to the end of the Twentieth Century (and sadly still alive and kicking), it still wasn't a true communication with the dog, and his particular wants and needs.

What does it do?

Leslie uses choice in her interactions with dogs. Dogs are allowed to make a choice about their care and comfort. And this doesn't always fit in with our expectations! *Look at That* is a method of offering the dog a choice over the response he's going to give to something that up to now he has found challenging and worrying. It has elements of counter-conditioning, but is a whole different conversation.

Let's look at your supposed fear of spiders again. If I say to you, "There's a big black spider over there, but here - have this piece of cake!" you, who are terrified of the beasties, are not going to want my cake. You'll stiffen, stand up, crane your neck, look directly at the spider - *you have to see where it is!* You have to assess the level of threat and work out your escape route. You'll push me and my cake aside so you can see clearly. You fear that if you take your eyes off the creature, it'll grow bigger and bigger while you're not looking, then run up your back! You need to look at it.

238

So with your dog. If she sees something that frightens her, *she has to look at it!* It's no good trying to distract her, holding a treat to her nose as she bobs her head away so she can still look. She needs to assess the immediate level of threat. If she stays staring at it, though, she can become fixated. Staring at another dog or person is - as we've seen in Book 1 - very rude and challenging. It also intensifies the dog's emotions. So we need to interrupt this stare - without preventing the dog from her essential study of the fear object.

We mark the dog for looking at the scary thing, then reward her so that she has to turn her head to get the treat. Now she's free to look again. Repeat, repeat, repeat, until your dog has finished gathering the information she needs, she dismisses the thing from her mind, and wants to engage with you and the world again. I'll take you through a training program in the next chapter, and there's a video in the Resources section that will show you *Look at That* in action: you'll see just how powerful it is.

We are changing the dog's head from reactive to passive. She's able to look at the fear object without reacting. She's thinking. She'll gradually learn that when she looks at anything in the context of this game, she will never have to interact with it. It puts her into a bubble where she is safe. She doesn't have to make those difficult decisions about whether she should use fight or flight. She doesn't have to work out a response with all its ramifications and consequences. This becomes a game she can rely on to produce treats *and* keep her safe.

Because she has to turn her head to get the treat she's earned, you break the stare. This will make life easier for whoever was being stared at, and will help to reduce your dog's anxiety. Her staring will become less and less intense, till she's able to just chuck a glance at the thing that you are "LATting": she has accepted its existence and is no longer afraid of it.

As you'll see, you can use *Look at That* for anything that your dog reacts to, be it a person, a dog, many dogs, dogs running, joggers, roadworks, children screaming, bikes, cars - you-name-it. You encourage your dog to look calmly at the thing that's worrying her rather than have a knee-jerk reaction to it. Once she's had the opportunity to study it without getting upset, she'll usually be able to move on. And she learns a new skill - to be able to reflect before acting, to reduce her impetuous responses, to become thoughtful and make good assessments of the situation.

Life has just got a whole lot calmer! For both of you.

In this chapter we have learnt:

- The origins of *Look at That*
- What it can do for you
- That we have a new way to converse with our dog!

Chapter 4
Look at That: how to teach it

When you are working to alter your dog's response to something she would usually react to, it's critical that your dog learns it as a fun game with you. So you would not start teaching it out in the wild world where things are constantly alarming your dog! The context of the learning will affect your dog's feeling about this game ("Oh-oh, something bad is coming …"). So I like to start this in the house, using something that the dog is happy to see.

Usually this will be your partner or mother or sister or friend - someone your dog likes and is familiar with in your home - but my Rollo the Border Collie learnt it while looking out of the window at his beloved chickens!

You'll be using your marker word "Yes!" or if you prefer you can use a clicker to teach this. When using it for real you'll seldom have a clicker in your hand at the precise moment a strange dog appears up ahead, so it's probably better to stick to the vocal marker. Your dog is already very happy with your Yes and knows that this means a treat is forthcoming, from the games in Book 2, Lessons 3-5. Her head should turn very quickly to your treat.

Lesson 8: Look at That

1. Have your dog on a loose lead beside you, say on your left
2. Have your helper move out of sight - perhaps the other side of a doorway

3. Be ready with a treat in your right hand
4. Your helper steps into view
5. Your dog looks towards the movement that has caught her eye
6. "Yes!" you say instantly, as she looks at your helper, instantly recognising that this is not a threat, just interesting
7. Quickly take the treat to her nose and move her head round towards you - so she's no longer looking at your helper - and give her the treat
8. Repeat

After only a few repeats your dog will respond to your Yes and turn her head for the treat which you always give to her side. In fact, she'll start to become relaxed about your helper and start focussing on the treat. You don't actually want this! So your helper may have to become more animated - jump through the doorway, or knock on the door, or toss a toy in the air - anything to get your dog to glance towards him. Now you can say Yes and give her her treat.

Watchpoints

- You are rewarding your dog for <u>looking at</u> your helper, *so it's essential that you mark the moment she looks*, then give your treat as her reward. We want her to look!
- The key to working with this method is that *you* are as calm as you wish your dog to be. Some trainers have dismissed it as being over-stimulating and getting the dog more excited, not less so. They're doin' it wrong!
- Your words and actions are calm, quick, quiet, and efficient. This should all happen very fast.

You will find that at some stage your dog stops looking at your helper entirely and wants to focus on you and your treats. You will be able to judge whether she's seen enough to form a good opinion of the situation. If so, you can move off.

And it's usually at this first lesson that people desperately want to tell the dog to look - they want to feel in control. Remember we're working with choice training here. So it's the dog who will initiate this game - simply by looking at whatever has caught her eye! This is known as an environmental cue - something in the environment triggers the dog's action. There's no need for you to interfere and say anything other than Yes - the split second she looks at your helper. You only have one word to say - so make sure you say it at the right time!

Adding a vocal cue

It is useful, though, to have a vocal cue for later on. If you remember from Lesson 5 in Book 2, we added the word "Sit" as a label to describe what the dog was doing at that moment. Dogs don't have a verbal language, but they are acute listeners, and very quick at pairing a sound with an action.

So once your dog is playing *Look at That* quickly and well, you have time to slip in your vocal cue "Look at that!" just as she turns her head to look. Follow this with a quick Yes and treat, so you keep the rhythm and flow of the game. You don't have to say your cue every time - just when you have the opportunity you can add it sometimes to describe her action of looking. I'll show you how you can use this cue in the next chapter.

ACTION STEP 32

Teach *Look at That* and practice it whenever you can till it becomes a fluent and happy game for your dog. You can start taking it on the road by saying Yes whenever your dog spots something *of which he is not afraid*. This could be a car turning out of a side road, a person crossing the road, a cow mooing in a field - choose things your dog does not normally react to. Only gradually, and at a great distance, will you start using it for real.

In this chapter you have learnt:

- How to teach *Look at That*
- The finer points to watch out for
- How to add a vocal cue

Chapter 5
Taking *Look at That* on the road

When to use it

Once you have this game under your belt, you can use it at any moment when you or your dog sees something that may worry him. By initiating the LAT game you are putting the feared object into a structure that keeps it at bay and under control. You may just have time to do two Yeses and treats before heading off cheerily in the opposite direction. Your object is always to have a calm dog, not one that erupts all over the place. So if you can get in there with a couple of Yes-treats you are achieving this.

It's a very useful tool to use when something suddenly appears - whether at a distance or close to - a dog appearing from behind a car, for instance. A quick jump into the game while you plan your exit will make this transition smooth and trouble-free.

When not to use it

Sometimes a hazard - perhaps Number 1 on your dog's list of feared things, maybe a black dog (horrors!) or an old man with a stick (Noooo!) - will appear just too close and too suddenly for you to be able to do any more than your Emergency Turn (Key Lead Skill no. 6 from Book 2) and a sharp disappearing act. Remember to make as if you intended to do this anyway - keep it light and fun, even if inside you are churning!

Another time when it's not going to work is when your dog spots something, you say Yes and offer your treat - even holding it at your dog's nose as he stares - and he is unable to disconnect and take his treat. This means one thing: you are too close! Make distance immediately and see if you can try again from further away.

What was it that disabled your dog? It could have been a black dog *and* an old man with a stick, both at once! (See Book 2 on Trigger Stacking.) Or perhaps the dog was returning his stare, and adding in some threatening body language - or the old man was brandishing his stick and shouting. It was all simply too much. Time to make tracks fast.

Your vocal cue, and more

You've successfully added "Look at That" as a vocal cue when you want to initiate the game. When would you use it?

We have a height advantage, so we can often see things our dog can't. (If you're not sure if he can see it, bend over till your eyes are at his head level. Surprising what they can't see!) If the thing you've spotted is one you know may cause a reaction in your dog when it moves into his view, this is a great time to use your cue.

"Look at that," you say.

"Look at what?" wonders your dog as he peers into the distance, scanning for what you're asking him to look at. As soon as he clocks the thing, Yes, treat - you're into the game! A few treats and that black dog that would have caused an outburst from your dog has come and gone - without a murmur.

Now you can get creative. Lacy has a number of different cues for *Look at That* because she can react to a number of different things if they appear without warning or approach us. We have "Where's the dog?", "Where's the cat?",

"Where's the horse?", and "Who's that?" for people, as well as "Look at that" for an all-purpose cue. She already knows the words "dog", "cat", "horse".

So if we are in an area where there a number of things happening - dogs running, cyclists, children playing - and I spot a lone person talking into his phone and gesticulating with his arms as he walks (a sure trigger for Lacy) - I can say, "Who's that?" and Lacy will look for the ne'er-do-well I must have seen. She'll pick him out of the crowd, then a few Yeses and treats will despatch that person as a threat. Lacy is back in her bubble and safe to continue.

Listen to That

And you can use this exact same technique for something your dog can hear but not see! It may be the sound of roadworks outside, a dog barking in the distance, a helicopter overhead, a sudden shout …

If you want to use a cue, the same "Look at that" will suffice. Remember that dogs don't have the same verbal language as we do, and to your dog, "Look at that" means "Study the thing that may worry you and know that it won't hurt you". You don't need to get into the semantics of verbs!

The magic of this game!

The true magic of this game will unfold with use. Not only can you use the cue to pick out hazards at a distance before your dog sees them, but the time will come when your dog initiates the game herself!

On a walk one day, Lacy started to stare down the hill and urgently back to me, down the hill and back to me. I followed her gaze and saw some riders there, gathering their horses for a gallop up the hill. I called Lacy to me and started the Yes-treat cycle. The horses galloped past us - only ten yards away - and on up the hill. By the time they had gone and we stopped the game,

Lacy was so pleased with herself! She had spotted the horses, and instead of starting to worry about how she should react - whether she should bark at them or chase them - she engaged with me in a game she has come to trust to keep her safe *and* keep her topped up with cheese. Our walk continued in peace.

In this chapter we've looked at:

- When and when not to employ *Look at That*
- How to communicate better with your dog
- The joy of seeing your dog taking over the initiative and choosing to start the game

Section 3

Behavior Adjustment Training aka BAT

Chapter 6
What is it?

BAT was devised by Grisha Stewart. Like Leslie McDevitt and many of us involved with working to help growly dogs, she had a dog who was afraid of many things, including people and children. The existing methods for dealing with reactive dogs were unacceptable to her, as they mostly relied on blame, force, and often punishment - however subtle, it's still punishment (see Book 2) - which serve only to shut the dog down and remove his warning signs. It does not change the underlying emotions.

So she developed a system which empowers the dog to make his own decisions and learn how to cope with his fears. As in all choice training, we support good decisions and set things up so that the dog is unlikely to make a poor decision. And if he still does make a poor choice, we have ways to remove him from the situation quickly and painlessly.

I was trained by Grisha and was among the first few Certified BAT Instructors in the UK. So I've worked with her and seen first-hand the principles that govern her actions.

And like her, I'm passionate about empowering the dog: I don't do things *to* my dog, I do things *with* my dog. Wherever possible - every day, in every way - my dog is given a choice. And BAT encourages good decisions. When these good decisions are made repeatedly from a safe distance and without interference, they gradually become the default response of the dog. Food is used little in BAT - we want the dog to get his rewards from being free to interact with his environment, and encourage natural dog activities like sniffing and exploring.

"I can't believe it!"

People are often amazed at their dog's ability to make good decisions when he is free to do so. I frequently get comments like "I'm really impressed! I thought he would be a nightmare," after their first outdoor BAT session. The system builds the owner's trust in their dog, the dog trusts that the owner won't lead them into trouble: everyone relaxes!

BAT has similarities with Look at That - but in the case of BAT we work in a way that minimises our intervention. In other words, the dog is the decider here - we are only going to intervene if he needs to be fished out of trouble. This goes against a lot of what people think when they first arrive at a course. They feel they should be doing more; they should be manipulating their dog with the lead; they should be controlling their dog. In fact, the opposite is true! And once people "get" this, they find a new way to enjoy being out and about with their dog. They are no longer the minder of an unpredictable and baffling animal, they develop a team approach to the world and its wonders (and hazards). They can sit back and watch their clever dog work it all out.

The joy of BAT is that you can use it for anything the dog finds frightening - dogs, people, horses, children, traffic, quick movements, hang-gliders (we get a lot of aerial invasion where I live, on the side of the Malvern Hills), black shiny rubbish sacks, motorbikes, strange noises ... and so on. In Grisha's latest BAT bible (see Resources section), you'll find a piece I wrote about one dog's terror of traffic transforming quickly and painlessly to a comfortable tolerance.

We'll be looking at some of those applications in the upcoming chapters. But first you'll need to know what you need for a successful BAT session, and we'll look at that next.

In this chapter we have learnt:

- The origins of BAT
- That honouring your dog is so much more effective than controlling him
- Whatever your dog's particular *bètes noires,* things will change, for the better

Chapter 7
Effective BAT essentials

Lead Skills

These are of the first importance. Without these you are going to make life a lot harder for yourself. While I'd like you to revisit all the Key Lead Skills in Book 2, I'm going to assume that you have grasped numbers 1 and 2, and reproduce here the ones you specifically need for BAT. And if you jumped straight to Book 3 this chapter is even more important.

Keeping your hands soft

Keeping your hands soft on a floppy lead can be hard to do. You've spent ages holding the lead tight as if your life depended on it, restricting your dog's freedom. This is understandable as you may have been afraid he would hurt someone.

But now we want the dog to have freedom - freedom to choose to stay calm! - and making sure you keep your hands soft and the line loose is going to go a long way towards this. If your dog sails off away from you, you need to be able to stop him without yanking him off his feet. You want him to slow down, turn, and choose to come back to you. The lead needs to stay fluid so nothing sudden happens. Your grasp as you clutch the lead tight and the tension this causes will tell your dog that something bad is happening. Perhaps he'd better bark at the nearest thing to keep it away!

I know you're thinking that if you loosen the lead, he'll pull all the time - but that's the old thinking. You now know that giving your dog the freedom to choose and then rewarding the choice you want will have him making good decisions in no time. As he learns these new skills, things will be changing dramatically before your eyes. Don't worry about your seeming loss of control: you will always have a firm hold of the handle.

Key Lead Skill No.3
Holding the handle safely and flaking the line

Whatever lead or line you are using (and please don't use one less than 6 feet in length!) you need to hold it safely. Safe so that your hand can't slip out, and safe so that your wrist can't get broken if your dog suddenly lurches out at an angle.

Holding the handle safely

1. Hold the lead handle up in one hand - say, your left hand - while the other hand - your right hand - goes through the loop like threading a needle
2. Then, while the handle is round your right wrist, bring the lead up and grip it against your right hand with your right thumb.
3. The line is now emerging from between your thumb and hand. This way you have a secure hold without stress, and your bones are safe!

If this has totally confused you (sorry), you will be pleased to know that there is a video illustrating this and the following lead skills which you'll find in the Resources section.

Safety point: if you insist on letting your children handle your reactive dog, then they should not hold the lead this securely - far safer for them if they simply hold the line and ignore the handle so they don't get dragged across the road. But seriously: don't.

Long line skills

For a lot of the training you'll be learning, you'll need to use a long line. Panic not! It's very easy when you know how. I find that people - once introduced to the joys of the long line - never want to go back to a shorter lead, except, of course, on the street.

This long line is not going to trail on the ground - it's going to stay in your hands, free of mud and wet, and is not going to wind your dog's legs up in knots or be a trip hazard for you or any passing children. You can watch the video in the Resources section, and I'll describe it for you here too.

A long line of about 15 feet is perfect for our purposes - see Book 2 for what to choose. It will provide a connection between you and your dog while allowing her to mooch around in a natural manner, and - importantly - give her the freedom to express her body language. You will always have a safe hold of the handle and a lot of the line, but you can allow your dog to make choices. Don't worry, we'll make sure these are all good choices! Just like the red or blue jumper offered to your toddler, we will limit the range of choices she can make, and weight the best choice heavily in our favour.

So the first thing to learn is how to control that line without breaking your fingers, or causing your dog to be yanked to a halt. This system is known by the nautical term "flaking" - used when the line is laid out on the deck in figures of eight. This ensures that when the net is thrown overboard, the line runs freely and there is no danger of a knot stopping the net from deploying, or of a coil catching a sailor's leg and taking him overboard with it.

You may be in the habit of winding a rope up in loose coils. The danger of this is that if your dog suddenly shoots forward, a coil will close round your fingers. There is a very real danger of breaking a finger this way!

Flaking the line

1. Layer your line, in the hand holding the handle, in long bows or figures of eight.
2. As your dog moves away, you can open your fingers for the line to snake out through the channel your other hand is making, then as you and your dog near each other again,
3. you can flake it into your hand again so it's not touching the ground.

All these lead skills really become very easy with a bit of practice - even for people who have difficulty distinguishing left and right, or who are not very nimble-handed. The long line will become a soft and relaxed connection between you and your dog. It will shrink and grow organically as your dog moves closer to you then further away again. It's like gently holding a child's hand, rather than gripping that hand tight as you might if you were near a busy road with a fractious four-year-old.

Whoa there!

So let's look now at how you can slow your dog to a gentle halt without pulling. You really never have to pull your dog's lead again!

Key Lead Skill No. 4
Slow Stop

1. Your dog is heading away from you, perhaps in pursuit of a good scent, or trying to reach someone.
2. As he moves away from you, loosely cup your left hand under the lead, letting the line run through freely, gradually closing your grip so he can feel this squeezing action as the lead slows down.
3. This will slow him sufficiently to ease him into a stand.

CALM WALKS WITH YOUR GROWLY DOG

4. Now relax your hands and lead - you may need to take a small step forward to let your hands soften and drop down - and admire your dog standing on a loose lead.
5. You can attract him back to you if you need to with your voice - treat, and carry on.

This should all be calm, mostly noiseless, and easy. It's like holding your friend's hand and gently slowing them down till they come back into step beside you. No need for "Oi!" "Stop!" "C'me here" or anything else other than saying, "Good Boy!" and giving him a welcoming smile when he reorients to you.

Try this first with another person instead of your dog to help you. Ask them to hold the clip of the lead in their hand, turn away from you and let the lead drape over their shoulder, with you behind them holding the line. As they walk away and you start to close your fingers on the lead, they should be fully aware of that sensation and respond to it. They'll be able to tell you very clearly if you're gently slowing them or jolting them to a stop! Your dog too will recognise this feeling on the lead as "Oh hallo, we're stopping now."

When you start, it may take a few attempts to get your dog to stay still and balanced when she stops so that you're able to relax the lead. After a while she'll know that this rubbing sensation on the lead is the precursor to a halt. The right sort of harness will help enormously to get her to balance on her own four feet instead of using you as a fifth leg. See the Resources section at the end of the book.

You may find that your dog slows beautifully to a halt, but as soon as you relax your line she surges forward again! So when you slow stop her, relax your hands just a little (an inch or so) to test whether she's standing balanced on her own feet. If she immediately starts to lean forward again, ease her to a stop again - maybe just using your fingers on the line - and test again. Sooner or later, she's going to realise that slow stop means stand still. The point to remember is that if you've decided she should stop (you may be seeing trouble up ahead) then stop she shall. Don't move yourself once you've committed to stopping.

But what if stopping is not enough?

There are going to be times when you can slow stop your dog, but she is still trying to surge forward. Maybe you're just too close to the thing that's worrying her. So, as you know from Section 2, Chapter 3 of this book:

Whenever your dog is unhappy about a situation, the first thing to do is make distance.

But how can you do that? You know that if you try and haul her back when she's this aroused that it's going to turn into an ugly mess. Not only is it hard to drag her backwards - her feet are firmly planted behind her and you're pulling against her strongest muscles, in her back and haunches (think of a horse drawing a cart) - and worse, just trying to pull her back is highly likely to trigger an outburst.

You are going to love this lead skill! Instead of trying to force her to comply with what you want, remember the red and blue jumpers! Give her a choice!

Key Lead Skill No.5
Stroking the line

1. Hold onto the line and stay put yourself to make sure your dog can't move forward
2. With a hand-over-hand action you *gently stroke* the line as you make attractive cooing and kissy noises. There is NO pulling going on
3. Your dog will feel this gentle touch and turn to look at you, as you bend over behind her in a kind of play-bow inviting her to join you.

4. She'll turn of her own volition and trot happily towards you, the scary thing quite forgotten.
5. Back up a few steps while she engages with you, then you can turn and head away.

It's as easy as that. And people are usually astonished when they learn this skill! Make sure you have the other skills down before you start on this one. Once you have mastered this, along with the other skills you've learned, *you will never have to pull your dog's lead again.* Think of that!

Most of you will have some experience with children, either through having your own, or through having been one. Think of the times you've needed to distract your child - possibly from a dangerous situation - by saying "Is that a *giraffe* over there?" or some such. You get a lightning response! This is the same kind of idea we're using here. Distraction and diversion.

All these lead skills can be done with a short or a long line. I find that it's easier to learn the first two on a short line, and these three here on a long line. Once you've mastered them, you can use them with any lead. For BAT we'll be working on a long line.

It's you who has to do some learning here. Just like driving a car, if you grate the gears and stamp on the pedals your car is not going to perform well. To get a smooth "drive" with your dog, you're going to need to learn these Key Lead Skills carefully. Your dog will say, "Oh, that's what she wants!" and it will all become a breeze. You really will wonder how you managed before!

Whatever lead skill you choose to use at any time, your first response is always: relax, soften hands, drop your shoulders, b-r-e-a-t-h-e.

A "Stuffy"

A what?? I always like to start any BAT training off using a stuffed toy dog. It needs to be a realistic, life-size dog - and there are some great ones available (see Resources section). If you're lucky you can pick one up at a charity shop or car boot sale. Or your teenage daughter may have something lifelike that will do the trick.

Why use a stuffed dog - surely the dog will know it's not real? Actually no, they don't. They are totally convinced. The reason for using a stuffy to start with is that the handler has to learn this new system, and the dog has to learn this new system. I don't need to add something unpredictable into the mix! I know that the stuffy will stay where he's put, and that he'll behave nicely (my stuffies all have identities: there's Melissa, Dave, and Killer, and Puss and Pusspuss the cats). The novice handler can focus entirely on their own dog and - crucially - their line-handling skills. The aim is not to go and meet Dave or Melissa (don't recommend meeting Killer), but just to tolerate their existence in the landscape.

Using a stuffy also helps *you* to relax. You may have spent years walking your dog in a state of heightened awareness, waiting for the ghastly moment when he kicks off. Once you can focus entirely on your dog and not on what anyone else thinks, change suddenly appears possible.

You may feel self-conscious about other people's opinions if they come across you walking around near a toy dog. But hey - they're only going to think you a bit odd (if they notice at all: most people also think the toy dog is real). Isn't that better than their superior disapproval when they see you trying to control a "dangerous" snarling lunatic on the end of your lead?

Where will we be doing BAT?

You'll need a suitable place to start teaching BAT. This needs to be an open space where you can see a good distance. You don't want things jumping out at you all over the place and catching your dog unawares. This does not necessarily exclude towns and streets. If you are using your local park, you'll need to choose a time when it's fairly sparsely populated. You may find you can get access to one of those splendidly landscaped business parks out of hours, or the grounds of an educational establishment. A large and empty shopping centre car park could work well. Think distance. Choose your place carefully, with your own dog's fears in mind.

Also think what your dog's fears are. If she's afraid of traffic, clearly you'll start a long way from any road. If people without dogs are upsetting, choose a place where you're unlikely to see lone people - taking a shortcut home from work through the park, for instance.

In this chapter we have:

- Revisited the vital Key Lead Skills you'll need to be fluent with
- Looked at the approach you need to adopt
- Looked at suitable places to start out

Chapter 8
Let's get started!

Mabel studies Dave at a safe distance

You've got your harness; you've got your long line; you've got your stuffy; you've found a great place to start work with your dog. Now what?

When you're doing a BAT session, I want you to remember two things:

1. Whatever your dog wants to look at is what you are working. So if he needs to study the dogs playing 200 yards away, or the helicopter

overhead, instead of the stuffy at 40 yards, then that's what you "BAT".

2. The object of the session is not proximity to the trigger - whether stuffed or real. The object is to have a calm dog. If you spend twenty minutes wandering around in the area of your trigger and your dog stays calm and doesn't react - that's a successful session! Anyone watching would wonder what on earth you are doing, as nothing appears to be happening. But we know that nothing happening is a good thing. Nothing happening is what we'd like on every walk! So always work at a distance at which your dog can remain calm - maybe alert and slightly challenged, but calm. It doesn't matter whether that's 30 yards or 200 yards. If the trigger needs to be a dot on the horizon before your dog can look and say "Ah well," before carrying on sniffing, this is where you begin.

A BAT session

I'm going to describe a typical first BAT session. As most reactive dogs will react to other dogs, we'll start there. I know there are a good number of dogs who are very happy with other dogs, they're just afraid of people, or men, or traffic, or just big lorries, or horses, or children, or just children playing - and so on. The system will be the same, and I'll help you with specifics later on. For now we're working with a standard-issue dog-reactive dog.

I'll choose a place to park Dave (or Melissa, or even Killer) where he's unlikely to be disturbed, and where I can move around him at a good distance. Ensure that your dog will not have his back up against a barrier of some kind - a wall, fence, hedge, or trees - this will make him anxious as he knows that retreat is impossible. You'll already be fairly well aware of the distance your dog needs to be able to observe another dog calmly. If it's 30 yards, start at 60. If it's 100 yards, start at 150. We are aiming for success!

Keep in mind the direction your stuffy is facing. Face-on is more threatening than tail-on. So start with it side-on to the direction you'll be coming from with your dog.

Now you can go back and fetch your dog. Load your pocket with some good smelly treats - just in case: I'll show you later what to do with these. Fit his harness, attach your long line to the back ring, gather up your line and start heading towards your stuffed-dog area. On the way, allow your dog to sniff and explore, paying the line out and reeling it in as needed to keep it off the ground, but loose. Keep a weather eye out at all times for incomers! If a real dog appears, you are now working that dog.

While there's nothing around, you can pay out some line to allow him to gather information about his new setting. You never want to be at the end of the line, bent double with outstretched arms grasping just the handle! Always have some line in hand so you can keep your arms slack and relaxed and remain upright and balanced yourself. If your dog is a mighty puller on the lead, you may need to stand slightly sideways, one foot planted ahead of you, and lean back slightly. If he is a lunatic puller, then take a turn of the line round your funnel hand (not the hand holding the flaked line) just till he settles a bit. That turn is easy to drop fast if you need to, and stops your hand getting burnt. You may want to wear some thin leather gloves for this lurching dog till he gets more used to the subtle restraint of the long line. Now you see the advantage of acclimatising yourself and your dog to the long line and its wonders way before you start a session.

Head in the general direction of your stuffy, being aware of what else is going on in the vicinity. Never go straight towards the trigger! Your dog can go anywhere he likes - and you will follow him - except straight towards the trigger. So go to the area at an oblique angle, as if you're going to carry on past, being sure to keep above the distance at which you know your dog can cope.

Your dog spots Dave

At some stage your dog will notice Dave (let's just call him Dave) and quite probably stop and stare. As soon as your dog looks at Dave, you slow-stop him and use just the gentlest finger-touching on the lead to ensure that he's standing on his own four feet and not leaning into the line. This is where all your practice with your partner or children pays off! Then *relax the line.*

KEY POINT: *Whenever your dog is looking at the trigger, you relax the line.*

We want him to look at Dave for as long as he needs to gather the information he needs, and we don't want to influence or interrupt that at all! So keep still and be patient.

Ideally, because your dog has spotted Dave from quite a distance, he's able to look, study, air-scent, listen ... then turn away and carry on walking and snuffling. "Good boy!" "Well done!" "You did it!" Plenty of encouragement from you for this big achievement - which he managed all by himself - as you follow him in any direction other than straight towards Dave.

Not so ideally, despite the distance, your dog is alarmed at the sight of Dave. He starts to get taller, stiffer, he's unable to balance on a loose line and leans into his harness, he closes his mouth ... these are all signs that he needs a bit of help to disengage.

If you were to pull him backwards, or shout, that would without any doubt set off a barking and lunging fit. So this is where you use your lead-stroking - which you have also practiced till you can do it in your sleep and your dog loves it. Step out a little so you're in your dog's peripheral vision, stroke the lead, make happy kissy noises, and as he turns to you tell him how delighted you are as you back up, then turn and walk away together. Your next glance at Dave will be from much further away - maybe even double the distance.

You'll notice that in these sessions - as in life - there is no room for "No," "Ah-ah," a raised voice, all of which will have the opposite effect to the one you want. You'd be adding fuel to the fire.

You are now continuing your easy shamble about the area, and relaxing your dog by letting him mooch around at a safe distance from Dave, before getting any nearer. You can always take breaks in your session, especially if your dog is finding it hard (hint: are you too close?). A break could be sitting down in the grass for a nuzzle, or playing Find it! with some of those super treats you brought with you.

Find it!

Usually in a BAT session, we don't use food. Why? Because you want your dog to relax and focus on his environment - not your pocket! If he's used to being trained for rewards, he may start to offer you some tricks or eager sits to get you to part with the treats. We don't want this. But using treats can be very useful as a distraction and to re-set him into snuffly, relaxed mode. This is especially effective if your dog has been stressed, got too close, had another dog run up to him, or had a barking and dancing episode.

1. First make distance from the things that are worrying him.
2. Then take several treats and whiffle your hand through the grass in front of your dog, saying "Find it!" and shedding treats as you go.
3. Your dog will now enjoy hunting down those treats.
4. Make sure you always drop several so he gets into the habit of continuing to hunt.

Working with heart monitors has shown that the dog's heart-rate plummets as soon as he starts sniffing and hunting. This is a natural, rewarding, thing for him to do. And it has the added benefit of being a calming signal to any other dog - which is also calming to him (see Book 1).

Carrying on with Dave

So, always keeping your distance in mind and only closing it slowly and subtly, wander around the area containing Dave again.

Every time your dog glances at the stuffy you will pause him, relax your hands, and slacken the line.

As he looks away to carry on walking, congratulate him warmly. Every time he can look at Dave without reacting makes it more likely that he can look at things and not react in the future. Every time he does react he's keeping this poor response at the ready - so make sure you keep him in the calmest possible state of mind for the whole session!

Remember, we're not looking to reach Dave. We're aiming to teach our dog that he can share a space with and look at something that would usually frighten him, *without needing to react.*

After you've been ambling past Dave for a while, getting ever so slightly nearer as you go (but never closer than ten yards or so), perhaps walking all the way round him so that your dog can take a safer look at him from behind, you can close your first session and call it a day. You could trot off back to the car with your dog - you may want to play Find it! with him on the way to help him unwind. He will be tired - he's worked hard - so ensure plenty of sleep and rest for the rest of the day.

Don't forget to go back and fetch Dave! And hide him in the car again - where your dog can't see him - ready for your next session.

This first session may take twenty minutes or so. Many short sessions will work better than occasional mega-sessions.

Looking back over the session

After your first attempts at BAT, you may be marvelling at how calm your dog is able to stay - now you know how to help him. And helping him means, largely, getting out of his hair and letting him work things out for himself. You are always on hand if he runs into trouble. You may have seen him getting in a little too deep, and if you weren't quick enough to help him out he may have had an outburst. But you now know how to respond to that to help those whirling hormones to settle again.

All in all, while you watched your dog finding new ways to respond to the world, you should have felt your own confidence growing during the session. One handler of a dog who was terrified of people said to me after her first outdoor BAT session: "I felt a great weight slide off my shoulders."

Troubleshooting

Let's have a look at some typical queries that can come up:

I'm getting tangled up in the line

Try some more practice with a helper playing the dog. Then try with your dog playing the dog. If you're all fingers and thumbs, you could attach the clip end of the lead to a chair in the kitchen, then practice moving away and back, turning this way and that, always keeping the line comfortable in your hands.

I get burnt by the line

Try the solutions suggested in this chapter for lunatic pullers. But be sure you have the right sort of line. A good one is inexpensive, so please don't mess around with a length of heavy rope you found in the garage! I favour flat webbing with a soft woven edge, ¾" wide will be fine for small to medium dogs, 1" wide for a big dog. Rope is often too bulky to handle, and if it's fine it's likely to burn. It also absorbs a lot of water and becomes very heavy in the rain. If you find a very soft-woven rope of ½" or so it may work.

You say to keep the line loose - but when we start out he's pulling like a train! It's impossible to keep it loose.

Practice your long line work away from your BAT session. Your dog needs to learn some manners and not pull so hard into the harness. You may find that teaching him Loose Lead Walking will help. See *Let's Go! Enjoy Companionable Walks with your Brilliant Family Dog,* the third in the **Essential Skills for a Brilliant Family Dog** series of books, in the Resources section. For now, in your practice sessions, keep a firm hold on the line and don't advance if he's pulling hard. He'll gradually become softer and lighter on the line.

How do I know when he's looked for long enough and is ready to move?

Your question is good, as you don't want to interrupt your dog before he's done. There are lots of signs you can look out for, and you'll gradually get quicker at spotting them. Your dog may give soft slow blinks towards Dave, he may open his mouth again (especially if of a breed that often has an open mouth, like Border Collies or German Shepherds). He may look away with his head then turn back to study Dave again. He may look at some dogs running in the distance, then check Dave before moving on. He may sniff the ground, turn his body away, relax his shoulders or change his stance. Just before turning away, many dogs will flip their ears back to check the path is clear. This is a good sign for you to be ready to move off with your cheery "Good boy!".

I don't notice other dogs rushing in till it's too late!

It can be hard to take in your surroundings at first when you're focussing so hard on your dog to spot his every signal. This is a skill you will develop, so take a friend with you for now, who can act as lookout. And when you see something coming at you? Just do your lead-stroking or Emergency Turn and happily jog off.

I'm not sure I'm doing it right.

Well, as you're a total beginner it's unlikely that you have it all perfect! Yet. Familiarity will make it flow better. Top tip! Have a friend video your session on a smartphone - you'll be amazed what you'll see that you never noticed at the time.

My dog zipped round behind me and nearly had me over!

Be sure you're always facing your dog. If he moves out to the side or behind you, then decides to take off, you're going to end up with a wrenched shoulder or a muddy backside! So turn and face him at all times, with your hands in front of you, not pulled out to the side.

When I pull him away because he's beginning to look fierce, he leaps up barking. It's a mess.

Don't! Don't pull him away. As I said earlier, this is usually guaranteed to trigger an outburst. This is the place for your lead-stroking (Key Lead Skill no. 5). Once you master this skill you will never have to pull your dog's lead again. That sounds so good I'm going to say it again: you never have to pull your dog's lead again.

What use is this? It's real dogs on the street he reacts to.

We are taking your dog out of the situation he finds scary in order to help him practice his social skills and body language in a controlled environment without stress. And to help you practice yours! Remember those spiders from Book 2: when you're in the grip of an emotion there's not much cool reasoning going on. We'll come to street situations in good time.

ACTION STEP 33:

Get yourself prepared, take a deep breath, and work your first BAT session!

In this chapter we have learnt:

- Two key things to remember about a BAT session
- How to structure and carry out your first BAT session
- That you'll feel very proud of your dog and yourself

Chapter 9
BAT set-ups and variants

Once you've worked through your first session, reflected on it, and watched the video if you took one, you'll have a better idea of where you are and what you're doing. Some of this can sound like gobbledygook when you read it! It's when you *do* it that it all begins to make sense and fall into place.

So be sure to "have a go" before trying to understand more detailed information. You could even try with a non-reactive, easygoing, dog. You'll still learn a lot about body language and how she interacts with her environment, even though not scared.

More work with Dave

You can carry on working with Dave for a few sessions if you like. You can give him a bright bandana or coat, or use a needle and thread to change the set of his ears or tail to ring the changes. And you can get a helper to go up and "talk" to Dave! Your helper can get Dave's tail wagging, have him jump up enthusiastically to greet him, laugh and enjoy his company. You may need to get a bit further away for this - but it'll sure rekindle your dog's interest in this boring, stationary, dog! All the time you are working Dave, your handling will be getting more natural and relaxed, and you'll be learning more about your dog's responses without fear of the other dog. It's well worth getting a stuffed dog to help out at these early sessions.

Remember to relax those shoulders, stay upright, soften your hands, and breathe.

Set-ups vs spontaneous BAT

While BAT should now become an automatic way of life for you and your dog - using it to cope with random objects of fear at a distance, even for one minute at a time - it can be helpful to arrange set-ups so you can work more thoroughly and for a longer time. So you can consign Dave to your teenager's bedroom and find yourself a person and a real dog. We're still looking at our standard-issue dog-reactive dog at this stage. This decoy dog needs to be socially-skilled and bombproof, but not your dog's best friend.

When using a real decoy dog or person, your priority is that all involved in the session must be absolutely happy to continue. This includes your helper and his dog. As soon as he or his dog is getting uncomfortable, then the session stops. It's important that you honour all dogs - not just your own!

Ideally, your helper should be familiar with what you're aiming to achieve, and knows not to stare at your dog, or allow their dog to stare at your dog. If you need to give your helper instructions on the fly, you can use mobile phones if the distance is too great to speak casually. A good helper is immensely valuable - not just to watch out for incoming hazards, but also to give you feedback after the session, such as, "Usually your dog stares then blinks and turns away. But the time he barked he didn't blink. He jammed his mouth shut and stared." You can't spot everything, and another pair of (informed) eyes is always helpful.

If this is an impossible goal, and you have no-one who can help you, then you will become more resourceful in finding times and places where your dog's triggers are likely to be found, in a low density, and with plenty of space for you to manoeuvre. We'll look at some possibilities in the next chapter.

It can be frustrating to set aside a time to work with your dog, you head to the place which is usually littered with people, or children, or dogs, and find … no-one. There's not a sinner out! See this is as a gift: a bit of comfortable, private time with your dog, where you know you're going to have a pleasant outing. You may be so relaxed by this, that when you go home and find you have to pass something usually considered alarming, you will have a positive experience.

Working through those triggers

Many reactive dogs have multiple triggers. So you could be looking out for people, dogs, bikes, joggers, children, traffic, you-name-it. But not all at once!

- One day you could choose a road junction with a low level of traffic, no people, and plenty of space to get away from the road.

- Another day you may walk along a road near a school at school-out time where you can watch children passing from time to time (gentlemen, take care with this one!).

- You could walk outside the fence of your usual dog park - this will give both of you great confidence as you can get slightly closer than usual in the sure knowledge that you are safe.

- You may notice when there is a local bike race or outdoor bike class, and position yourself safely away from it but where your dog can still watch the bikes.

- You could put Dave under a hedge or at the side of a quiet road so you can come across him and work him at a distance. You have the advantage of knowing exactly where he is and just what he'll do (nothing!).

- Joggers are often easy enough to find, but not so easy to avoid, as they will insist on running straight at your dog, expecting you to simply evaporate as they arrive (crash-bang, puff puff, arms flailing).

It's no surprise that some of these inconsiderate road-users get bitten. Get yourself right away from their likely running path, so they are running past at a distance.

- Always remember distance!

Whatever you're working against, whether it's in a set-up or taking advantage of some of the ideas listed above, you will always remember these things:

- Focus on your dog's response
- Measure success by his level of calmness not by proximity to the trigger
- Your distance will naturally diminish over time - don't push it

Some more tricks of the trade

I like to get my students to graduate from wandering around the decoy to something more like real life.

Parallel Walking

Once your dog has studied the decoy dog from a distance and is able to disengage easily and carry on his way, you can move to Parallel Walking.

1. *Keeping the same distance as before*, start to walk alongside your helper at a similar speed. You may be 60 yards apart to start off. There'll be less sniffing allowed here because you want to keep more or less level. You could use an ordinary 6' lead if you liked.

2. Go back and forth over 100 yards or so, turning at the same time, and allow the distance to gradually and naturally close between you. You may take a few sessions to achieve this.

3. When you are near enough, say 10 yards, you could start conversing with your helper. Chat about this and that, but always be aware of

what your dog is doing. If he's still sending a lot of glances towards your helper's dog, it's too soon to get any closer.

4.   You may eventually both stop and chat. Keep watching your dog. You could be 5 yards from each other. As long as both dogs are happy, go for it.

5.   If all the signs are good and you are confident of your dog's reaction, you could have a very short meeting - if both helper and helper dog want this. Your dog should make the first move forwards. Keep it very brief - just nose-to-nose for a couple of seconds - both of you moving around behind the dogs to make sure the leads don't get tangled.

No.5 is not a necessary step. It may be that your dog will take way longer to want to meet anyone or anything. Honour her choice! Maybe next month … Maybe next year … Only when she's ready.

Oppositional Walking

If Parallel Walking is going well over a few sessions, you could try Oppositional Walking - that is to say, you and your helper are walking towards and passing each other. You'll need to go back to a slightly greater distance to start this, as this is much more difficult for your dog.

Go back to the Dog Body Language section in Book 1 to refresh your mind on this vital information. You'll have a clear view of what your helper dog is feeling. An experienced helper dog is quite likely to switch sides as you approach so he's the far side of his handler. Interesting: perhaps you should encourage your dog to do the same.

Follow the same steps as above, but when you get to No.3 –

3.   Start to go in opposite directions, over 30 yards or so. You can make that distance longer if you feel it's too challenging for your dog. Your helper will ensure that his dog doesn't stare at yours - popping tasty

treats into his dog's mouth will usually do the trick to get him to focus on his handler instead of you.

4. Gradually close the distance between your paths.

5. Now this is getting much more like passing another dog on a road! Your dog is learning where to look and how to behave - all on your lovely loose lead held in soft hands.

6. You may want to stop (how far away should you be? You decide) and "ask the way" of your helper. This may involve him waving his arms to point. All good practice for your dog to ignore!

Keep in mind that you are still working in an open space, your dog knows he can escape in any direction. So when you move this to a quiet road, you could be on opposite sides of the road. Choose a more open road, without walls and hedges or buildings right against the pavement - always avoid those "tunnels"! You'll soon be able to pass your helper - perhaps saying Hi or Good morning as you pass. Only move to a more constricted area gradually.

Softly, softly, catchee monkey

"Gradually". I say it a lot. It's important to make haste slowly. Jumping forward may require you to go back several steps. You have the rest of your dog's life to work on this. One day you're going to say, "Wow! Last year we couldn't have done that!" It's a gradual change we're looking for - but your dog may surprise you by progressing faster.

Troubleshooting

My dog is fine until he's actually passed the other dog, then he spins round and tries to nip the dog's tail

You're too close! Way too close. Your dog is doing well to hold it together until he's passed the dog, but then he just wants to make sure that dog knows not to come so close again. Go back to a greater distance: "Can you do it here?" and only close the distance very gradually.

Why do I have to do all this? My dog just wants to play with the other dog!

If your dog is able to approach another dog calmly and have a pleasant greeting then either move on or have an appropriate game, then you don't. But you wouldn't be here if that were so. If you want to befriend someone, you don't start off by shouting and frightening them. It seems that your dog has some anxiety issues with regard to the other dog, and these techniques will help him to be able to approach a dog without doing his song-and-dance routine. Removing approaches from his walks for now can calm him sufficiently to enable good choices later.

My dog's ok with other dogs - he's terrified of traffic

Then you'll do your BAT training with traffic instead of a decoy dog. We'll look at this in the next chapter, but remember the principles are just the same. You are empowering your dog and giving him a choice - then honouring his choice.

My dog was mistreated by people, so he's afraid of them

Again, the same principles apply. In some ways it's easier because you can ask your helper to do just what you want - or not do what you don't want! Next chapter.

We were doing so well, then a dog came running in at us. I panicked and forgot what to do. Have I ruined everything?

No, you haven't ruined everything. Give yourself and your dog a break for a couple of days to let all the hormones settle - enjoy games at home. When you're ready you can start again, at a distance where you know your dog is comfortable. Rehearse your escape techniques in your mind (see Book 2). This is a good reason to practice your Emergency Turn frequently, so you can use it straight away when you need it. There are always going to be loose, rude, dogs. Learning how to cope with them is a big part of your strategy.

My dog is of a very barky breed. I find it hard to react before she barks

Those woofs can slip out very easily from a barky dog's mouth! It would be helpful to teach her *not* to bark, on cue. I start - at home - with rewarding them for barking when I ask for it, then I can reward them for quiet too. For many dogs "QUIET!" means that you're joining in with the noise and they should bark louder! You need to teach "Quiet" and connect it with … quiet. I'm not saying you interfere with your dog's response - just start from a greater distance and get your very quiet "Quiet" in as she's looking - quietly. This gives her a better chance of assessing the trigger and coming to a good conclusion. Having said that, you may find that a single woof escapes when she first spots the trigger then she's able to be calm while she studies it. A solitary wuff is acceptable. A cascade of woofs, not so good.

We start out well, then things get worse and worse

Well observed! The stress is gradually building in your dog and her coping skills are sliding away. Distance! Do some set-ups where your dog is never going to have to get anywhere near the object of her fear. If she does have a reaction, make more distance and play Find it. If she has two reactions, call it a day and start afresh another day. This is a marathon, not a sprint. In any case, don't you go getting anxious too!

In this chapter we have learnt:

- How to take BAT on the road and incorporate it into your daily life
- Gradual progress is the best way forward
- Your dog is going to surprise you - in a good way
- You are beginning to enjoy relaxing walks!

Chapter 10
More BAT variants

You've heard me say "distance" many times. You've heard me say "gradual". Keep those two words in mind whenever you're out with your dog. You should be thinking, whenever you step out of the door, of how you can find opportunities for your dog to excel. Short sessions all help.

Remember that road walks are specifically for training, not for exercise (see Books 1 and 2). "Today we're going to walk round the block without comment," you may be thinking as you set off on your walk - your dog in her comfy harness, a decent length lead, and pockets crammed with goodies. It may appear a simple goal for a walk, but (if you keep your walk short enough!) it's attainable.

The barking dog in the garden at no.11

The guardians of the gate

So it could be that you go for a walk around your neighbourhood and you decide that today is the day you're going to work the Barking Dog in the Garden at No.11. Usually you can only get past no.11 while dragging your screaming dog with you. Your aim is not going to be to breeze past no.11 in a happy cloud (though that will come later - really!) but to give your dog time, at a comfortable distance, to assess the Barking Dog. Keeping mindful of traffic on this road, give your dog plenty of line and let her just stand and watch no.11. When she breaks off and looks to you for guidance on where to go next, allow her to wander a few steps. If she's going towards no.11 slow-stop her and wait, with soft hands. Let her make the decisions about when and where she wants to move, and only intervene if you can see things are going pear-shaped.

During this session you may get within a couple of houses of no.11 without any bad reaction from your dog, the Barking Dog barking all the while. Maybe that's enough for today? Make a note of the tree or fence you reached, and start a bit further back from that tomorrow. Maybe you'll get a good few yards further without incident. And yes, one day you'll be able to walk past no.11 - probably on the other side of the road - with happy smiles and a carefree manner from both of you! I am always pleased and proud when I walk my four past a yapping gateway on our road. My group of four includes two reactors. They cast a glance towards the barkers and carry on trotting by.

If a friend wanted you to come to the edge of a 200-foot cliff to admire the view out to sea, you may be filled with terror at the thought. If he grabs you and drags you even one step nearer the edge you're going to panic, shout, pull back from him. If he lets you go and allows you to get on your hands and knees, perhaps you may crawl a little closer to the edge. Maybe you'll get a glimpse of the beautiful view, and feel able to crawl a yard nearer the next day. This is "gradual". Maybe that's as near as you'll ever get to the cliff-edge (you certainly wouldn't get me standing at the edge!) and that will do.

The view is not beautiful if you are terrified.

Somewhere different

Always look for new areas to practice your new skills. You want your dog to know that they will work anywhere. While you'll need to use your 6 foot lead when you're on the street, you can still handle it softly and gently and move *with* your dog rather than hauling him after you. Turning deliberately in a slow, tight, circle (you stay on the spot) with your dog on the outside can quickly alter a situation - even in a confined space. As soon as you're off-road again you can use your 15 foot line - which you're probably getting to love by now.

Keep your Emergency Turn (Key Lead Skill no. 6 from Book 2) well-polished and fun - it's always an exciting game. And get used to noticing escape routes as you walk, so they're in your mind if you need to move fast.

Stealth BAT

Ned calmly watches a frightening person at a safe distance (note soft line)

As you get fluent at switching straight into BAT the moment you need to, you can engage in Stealth BAT. This is where you see one of your dog's triggers appearing and take the opportunity to work it for a short while before it disappears.

So this could be a dog walking past on the other side of the road; it could be a lorry reversing round a corner, beeping; it could be children running; horses trotting by; a dog sitting waiting for his owner to stop chatting and move on; cyclists pedalling past; a person fighting to get an umbrella up; someone walking along the road talking into their phone and gesticulating weirdly (in your dog's opinion). You can make use of all these things to work a bit of BAT and give your dog some confidence about her environment. There's just one rule to remember here:

Be sure the object of your BAT session is happy about it

That doesn't mean you have to ask their permission first. It just means that if they notice you at all, they should not feel uncomfortable. This goes for people, children, dogs, horses - whatever. A person may even show a friendly interest in what you're doing. By all means engage in a quick conversation with them, but focus on your dog while you speak and be ready to move off as soon as you need to.

The over-friendly dog

Tigger the friendly pup has to learn to greet shy Django more politely

Your dog may be desperate to meet other dogs! He just lacks the social skills to do this politely and calmly. Some dogs seem to get stuck in a puppy-type approach to strange dogs - all leapy, licky, bouncy, paw-y - then give an older dog response when they don't know how to get away - snarl, snap, bark, lunge. They're frustrated by their inability to cope with the whole dog greeting thing. It can be that they fly in with good intentions, then panic when they get there and, not knowing how else to terminate the meeting, they snap to get the other dog away. Or maybe they just start singing and wailing when they see another dog and try to drag you over to them.

In this case, it's clearly when they first spot the dog that they need a bit of help. If you can interrupt the madly excited response and get some thoughtfulness and steadiness in, you can work on the actual greetings later on.

One way to keep this frustration from damaging your shoulder is to allow no greetings on-lead on a walk. This makes it clear to your dog that no amount of leppin' around and shouting will get him to the dog. You can restrict greetings to off-road areas when you still have the lead to help you. If your dog is off-lead when he spots another victim, this is a good place for the Collar Hold (Books 1 and 2), where the feel of the back of your hand against his neck will help to calm your dog, as well as restraining him if necessary.

Remember that we don't ever want to head straight towards the other dog. That applies equally in the case of the over-friendly dog. But when the dog looks, and you slow-stop him, you may wait forever for him to turn away, so fixated is he on the object of his desires. So this a place for Mark and Move. You simply mark - "Yes!" - his good calm behaviour (you may have to be very quick here!) when he first looks at the dog, and call him away as you head off. Yes - it's a little bit like Look at That. You can give a reward as you depart, to help with this. This uber-friendly dog is unlikely to be focussing on you for treats when there's *"A DOG!!!"* in the offing, so it's not going to interfere with his study of the dog, as it might well do for the dog who is afraid of other dogs and is keen to find a displacement activity.

Working this way, you can end up "tacking" towards the strange dog, like a sailing boat. Each time you stop your dog while he stares, you can move off in another direction - never straight at the dog. Eventually you *may* get to allow a greeting. Greetings should be very, very short. Just one sniff, then you mark and call and lead-stroke your dog away. If it went well, you can have another greeting, fractionally longer before you call him out. Always be sure to move around behind your dog so the leads don't get tangled! A sudden tightening of the leads could cause either dog to react. Perhaps after a couple of greetings the two dogs can be a little way apart while you chat to the other owner.

You want to take some of the fizz out of these over-excited stampedes towards another dog, and either the over-the-top greetings, or the panic-driven snap that can follow. Introduce some thoughtfulness into your dog while he learns some better dog manners.

Tigger gets it right!

In this chapter we have learnt that:

- A new life is opening up before you
- You can take every opportunity to build your dog's confidence
- You can now start looking for dogs, instead of avoiding them!

Chapter 11
Fear of things other than dogs

Fear of people

Purdey checks out Penny safely from behind

In some ways this is easier to work with than a fear of other dogs: you can give directions to your decoy person and control the situation better. But it can also be harder! When strange people are in the mix, they get the Dr. Dolittle complex and think that they'll be the one to break through this dog's fears on behalf of humanity. They can be very persistent. A long time ago that would have been me, before I knew better.

So you need to work with set-ups while *you* learn how to control passing people. I have worked with dogs who have been fearful of humans all their lives, and who - after just a couple of sessions - feel able to take them or leave them and not get into a panic. It is a wonderful thing to see!

You work BAT with your helper in just the same way as you start off with your stuffy. The only difference is that a person standing still would be weird - many non-fearful dogs would bark at that. So have your helper mooch around the area you want them in. They can gaze into the middle distance, they can stoop to pick a flower, they can pause and look at their phone. They can look out for incomers for you too. The one thing they can't do is stare at your dog. Naturally they need to be aware of where the dog is, but furtive glances will do. Having a dog-savvy helper, who has empathy for the fearful dog, will help greatly. If they're a long way away, you can communicate by phone rather than yelling.

Remember safety first. If your dog has bitten, chased and nipped, whatever - use a muzzle. Don't take any chances with your kind volunteer!

As your dog is able to wander about sniffing and relaxing and looking at the person occasionally in a calm manner, you can start - over a few sessions - to get your person more active. They can begin acting a bit more uninhibitedly. So they may take their coat on and off, swing it over their shoulder (they need to be observing your dog with soft eyes and quick glances so they do these things when she's watching), carry (apparently) heavy shopping bags, they may call out to an imaginary someone and wave, they may move their hands about while they talk agitatedly into their phone, they may sit or lie on the ground, they may jog or even run past you (at a safe distance from herding dogs!), they may get in and out of their car, they could even play the irrational drunk calling out a greeting to you. And they could drop their hat or scarf as they walk away, then your dog can study that carefully with her nose to get more information about its owner at a safe distance. Don't attempt all these things at once! Slow and steady wins the race …

If you can only use as decoy someone your dog already knows, they can have a variety of overcoats, hats, walking sticks and the like to disguise themselves and their walk. Remember we can recognise someone at a great distance just by their outline and their walk, so they'll need to limp, or walk slower or faster than normal.

You do *not* want your helper to try to interact with your dog, and definitely never to offer treats: this is very conflicting for a frightened dog. But you may end up with your fearful dog creeping close enough to sniff the back of the person (who's acting oblivious: "I see no dog."). For some dogs this would be a great triumph!

But remember your aim is not for your shy dog to become everyone's friend. That's not going to happen! Hopefully she'll relax more around your regular visitors and perhaps befriend them, but what you're looking for is an ability to tolerate the presence of strangers without feeling the need to do anything about them - neither barking ferociously nor running away in panic. See what one student had to say about her people-fearful dog after just two outdoor sessions learning BAT:

"We're really delighted with the improvements with Daf so far. We have just got back from a walk on the common and on Daf's terms walked round a big group picnicking and she paid them no attention at all. Hurrah!"

Note that she said "on Daf's terms". This shows a very solid understanding of what we are doing with BAT. It was Daf's choice exactly what distance she chose to pass the picnickers. Anyone watching would have noticed nothing - while Daf's owner burst with pride and joy at her achievement!

Allowing the dog to choose whether or not she wishes to interact with a person, and giving her full permission to totally ignore them is going to lead to a confident dog. She'll know that she never has to talk to any strange person, ever. You are seeing now the fruits of Action Steps 9, 17, and 24 - oft-repeated because of their extreme importance. *Show your dog that he never has to meet another person or dog ever again.*

I was surprised to come across Purdey - the terrified dog in the image at the top of this chapter - running off-lead with her jogging owner a few months after we had worked together. Purdey looked happy and relaxed and was clearly enjoying her outing. She was free to keep her distance and act normally while I spoke to her owner. When off-lead and running she had found that she didn't need to interact with anyone or anything - success!

There are many dogs who choose to avoid people in this subtle way. They may not be afraid, but they don't particularly want to talk to anyone. Do you want to talk to everyone you see on the street? They've worked this out on their own. Your people-fearful dog may need a little help to reach this happy state of independence.

Fear of Traffic

Meg ignores the traffic nearby

This is a fairly common fear in dogs who missed out on their early puppy socialisation - we looked at this in detail in Book 1. So any puppy who leaves the litter too late is at risk of this. So also are dogs who are reared on a farm, away from people and roads. This is one reason it's often found in Border Collies, who also have acute hearing and are bred to respond fast to movement. Whether you know the cause of this fear or not, we start from where we are.

Using the same BAT techniques we used for a strange dog, you can start with your dog at a good distance from the road, with just the occasional car, and with plenty of open space behind you so your dog doesn't feel hemmed in and panic. As always, start from a distance at which your dog is comfortable. When a car whooshes past along the road, let him look, on a slack line, then let him carry on in whichever direction he chooses. If he reacts - you're too close to the road!

When choosing your spot, keep in mind things which can exaggerate the experience:

- Rain - makes the cars much noisier
- Vertical surfaces bounce the sound back - tall buildings, walls, for instance
- Potholes or uneven surface - can cause cars to bump, bounce, and rattle noisily
- Bigger vehicles - buses, lorries, trailers
- Build-up of traffic - a continuous flow instead of individual vehicles
- A junction nearby that causes braking or noisy acceleration

So you may find your nice, friendly, carefully chosen area with the odd car pootling by suddenly becomes a speed track full of teeth and fury for your dog. You need to think on your feet! Move away.

Always default to distance first.

I like to start working with a traffic-fearful dog on a large expanse of grass and open land, with a distant road carrying individual cars (rather than a stream of traffic), so the dog can study each one. Gradually we work up to a junction with more of a flow of traffic - two or three vehicles at a time - but still plenty of open space to retire into whenever the dog needs a break. City streets would come much later. And walking along roads in the dark. A lot of dogs are afraid of the dark.

Negotiating a busy street

This can be hard for the reactive dog. All his fears are coming at him at once! You need to be continually aware of what he's seeing and what needs evasive action. You may think your dog is "fine" in the town centre - which surprises you when you consider his reaction to a single person you encounter on a less busy road.

But look at it this way: if an army brandishing sabres was bearing down on you, you'd lie low and hope they wouldn't bother with you - no point in fighting back. One person approaching - you just might be able to scare them off. Your dog may be creeping on eggshells while you think he's "fine". Do more BATwork with him so he can work out a new way to respond to what previously frightened him. Then you can re-introduce him to busier places a little at a time.

Troubleshooting

My dog just lies down. She's not afraid, she's just stubborn.

Oh oh oh. Dogs are not "stubborn". They don't do things to spite you. If she's lying down in the face of ... whatever it is that worries her, she's wanting to disappear through that hole in the ground we'd welcome when something upsetting or embarrassing happens to us. This is common in young puppies. She's telling you she is not comfortable about going any further. You need to find out just what it is she's afraid of, then try and isolate that trigger and work on it alone. If going for a walk means strange dogs, barking dogs, traffic, people greeting her, car doors slamming, children running about ... it's all too much for her. Give her a holiday from walks along that clifftop, relieve her of her "terror run", and start working through this book series from Book 1.

I can't always be training my dog - life goes on!

Indeed it does, but it doesn't necessarily have to involve your dog - until he's happy to take part. Once your BAT is going fluently, you can use it on walks with a shorter lead too. See a dog (person/jogger/car etc) and slow-stop your dog. Just stand with a loose lead and let him study the other dog. When he relaxes and glances at you to say "I'm ok with this," you can carry on walking. One day you won't even need to pause.

We had builders in, coming and going all the time. My dog's not mad about visitors so we shut him in another room, but he got out and bit a builder's bum. Have I now got to muzzle him at home?

Your dog is not mad about visitors, then he had to experience a veritable invasion! His stress levels were off the chart, and he was imprisoned as well. This is Trigger Stacking (Book 2) writ large. Get him used to meeting visitors again, on lead. Use Key Lead Skill No.2: Parking (Book 2) to ensure hands-off control. If he doesn't want to meet the visitor, let him choose to go in his crate or another room with something to chew to relieve the tension. And meanwhile work on People BAT at a safe distance outside the house. No, no need to muzzle him at home. The lead will keep your visitors safe.

My dog is quite happy to walk about the local shopping area with me in the daytime. But at night when it's nearly empty she'll bark at everything!

You're probably happy and relaxed walking about the shops amongst the bustle of mothers with pushchairs, old men with sticks, delivery men carrying parcels, cyclists, teenagers larking about after school, and so on. The busy-ness and mass of people is normal. But at night, that place is deserted. It's quiet. You see a person emerging from a doorway down the street: what's he doing? why is he there? is he a danger? Dogs are designed to notice things that are out of place. In a crush of people everything melds together. In the empty street, one person is out of place. And needs to be barked at!

My dog will sniff a new person, then jump back barking

Sounds as if it's all moving a bit fast for her. Perhaps the person moved, tried to stroke your dog, bent over, spoke, or - horror of horrors! - looked straight at her. Always allow your fearful dog to make the first move towards a person. And ensure that she has enough lead to move away behind you if she wishes. Teaching her the Carwash game (Book 2, Lesson 6) will enable her to find her safe place herself if she feels the need. If the person will do what you say, you can ask them to drop their hand down by their side for your dog to sniff. But they may do no more! Your dog can sniff their hand if she wishes, and come back to you. When you meet a stranger, you may shake hands with them, or just nod and smile. What would you do if they moved into your space, ruffled your hair, patted your bum (!), stared straight into your eyes? I don't know why dogs are expected to be people's playthings and tolerate stuff we would not tolerate ourselves.

In this chapter we've learnt:

- How to help the people-fearful dog gain confidence round people
- How to help your traffic-fearful dog manage in our busy, noisy, world
- To put ourselves in our dog's paws and see how it feels for us

Section 4

Putting it all together

Chapter 12
What do I use when?

So you've learnt four key methods for changing your reactive dog to a happier companion:

- Desensitisation and Counterconditioning
- Look at That
- Emergency Turn
- BAT

You are armed to the teeth with techniques - but which one should you use where? How to decide in the heat of the moment what you should do?

As a general rule, use the least intrusive method at any time. Keep out of the way and let your dog learn to cope and work things out for himself. But remember too, that discretion is the better part of valour! Be prepared to intervene to rescue your dog when it seems necessary. Don't wait till he's already anxious and barking.

Possible situations:

There are horses coming towards us, and their teenage riders are chatting to each other and not watching out!

Get out of their path and play Look at That till they've passed. Remember the story of Lacy and the horses in Chapter 5 of this book? When Lacy first saw horses she thought they were monsters from the deep that had to be chased away - this not helped by riders cantering straight past us with no warning. Now she sees them as a vicarious source of food, and no longer a worry.

Cyclists! There's a whole load of them heading straight at us.

You may be able to move off the road and post treats into your dog's mouth as they pass. If your dog won't take the treats, you're too close - make distance! Remember that the ability to take treats is a good gauge of your dog's state of mind.

The park is pretty empty except for a group of dog walkers on the far side

This is an excellent time to do a bit of Stealth BAT. You can gradually wander in a random fashion towards the other side of the park, with your dog making calm decisions all the while. You may even get within 20 yards of them before moving off after your very satisfactory session. Take care if the dogs are loose - they may run up to investigate. But if you can see their approach is friendly, and your dog has no history of biting, this could be the perfect time to have a greeting. After all, your dog has just spent at least ten minutes studying these dogs and hasn't felt the need to defend himself. Be sure your line is slack while they meet, keep behind your dog to avoid the line tangling with legs and necks, and stroke the lead and move off swiftly after a very short greeting. Very short? Say 5 seconds. Just your body movement may be enough to prompt your dog to come with you. If it went well, you can always have another greeting - perhaps another day.

I'm walking through the car park and a dog appears round the next car

Look at That would be my weapon of choice here. But if the dog looks as though it's come straight off your dog's personal "Wanted" poster of undesirable dogs, call out "Happy!" and go for the Emergency Turn instead.

As I walk through our residential area, dog walkers can come up behind us

Cross the road, then do some Parallel Walking with the other dog. This is no longer a situation to fear, but a situation to use as a training opportunity! Peel away if the other dog appears anxious.

I'm walking through town when a gaggle of small children cry "Goggie!" and wobble towards us, arms in the air.

Emergency Turn! And if they persist in chasing, ask the parents to call them back. The most stable dog could be alarmed by this! I was waiting for a friend outside a shop one time. After *three* Emergency Turns in the face of a shrieking toddler intent on "goggie-ing" Lacy, I was amazed to hear the father explain to his wife that he had to hang on to the child now because "that dog growled at her". Doting parents can be a danger to their children.

Incoming dog, with cries from the distant owner of "It's ok, my dog is friendly!"

This is the bane of many reactive dog owners' lives. See Books 1 and 2 for extensive escape methods. If it's too late and the dog has reached you, relax and back off while you prepare for your "House is on fire!" recall. I tend to call Lacy in and slip my hand into her collar, holding it very loosely but with the back of my hand reassuringly against her neck. Sometimes I ask both Lacy and Coco (the reactive members of my team) for a sit beside me - preferably off the path - till the other dog has gone by. An answer to "My dog is friendly,"? "Well, my dog is not." It may work, but it doesn't do to antagonise the other owner. Incoming wild dogs is a fact of life, and we have to learn how to cope with it, without panicking and making the situation ten times worse.

Don't get caught out when something happens. On your walks you can rehearse the various options: imagine the wobbly toddler, the galloping horses, the thoughtless jogger, and practice your technique then.

Troubleshooting

The moment she sees a strange dog - even at a distance - she starts barking. What do I do?

You have to slide your response in before the first woof emerges! You need to be very quick, notice the other dog first and be ready with your "Yes!". I'd choose Look at That here, to start with. If your dog is super-barky at the best of times you may allow one woof to escape as you mark and treat. After your dog has got over the initial fright, you may decide to move to BAT, possibly making distance all the while.

She doesn't bark and lunge any more, but she does stay staring at the dog for ages.

Fantastic progress! Very well done! The staring may be serving to intimidate the other dog - but it may also annoy him. When accompanied by calming signals, like blinks, lip-licks, and lookaways, it's also an indicator of how long your dog needs to assess the level of threat this dog presents – it's often very much longer than we allow. You can move away and let her study him from a greater distance. Practice your lead-stroking with your dog frequently as a game, so that her knee-jerk reaction to feeling movement on the line is to turn and face you. This can then become another of your handy interrupters. If you leave your dog staring for too long, she can get fixated and feel she has to do something. You don't want to head back to barking and lunging again!

When we pass a person close up - especially at night - just as they draw level my dog leaps up to grab them - help!

Don't pass a person close up! For now. If your dog has bitten then he should be muzzled when out. If not, try teaching your dog to wear a head halter (use the exact same technique for acclimatising to a muzzle - see Resources). This will give you control of the head, so if you are forced to pass someone within leaping distance you can shorten your lead and distract your dog.

"Happy!" has become such a favourite game that I can even use it to get a fast recall when he's off-lead!

That's great to hear! Repetition of these games - always as fun - is so profitable. Now you haven't just got a way to get out of trouble fast, you've got a new way to connect with your dog.

My dog's getting really quick at Look at That, so we tend to use that all the time

That's good that you find it so useful. But at this stage you need to be practicing all the techniques. They all work slightly differently, and you'll find a good time for each of them. Don't sell yourself short by opting for only one!

In this chapter you've learnt:

- When to apply your new skills
- To put them all together in your toolbox so you can pluck out the one you need in an instant
- Which techniques work best for you at this stage
- That keeping calm yourself is essential
- Distance, distance, distance - always distance!

Conclusion

We've arrived at the end of our journey through these pages. But it's not the end of the road for you and your dog - it's just the beginning!

If you've just read through these books for the first time, you're now ready to go back to the beginning, get the equipment you need, and start on the Lessons and Action Steps. You should find it all *even easier* to follow when you read it again. This is good. This means you are absorbing the information and letting it become part of how you think. The ideas are not novel and weird any more - they make sense.

By now you will be viewing your dog through new eyes. You will feel for him. You'll understand why he's doing what he's doing, and how you can help him make better choices and give both of you a better life.

And you'll understand why Choice Training is the way to go. It's the way we work with our family and friends, and what's your dog if not both family and friend? Using Choice Training will affect every part of your life with your dog. So much stress and strain and so many of those little daily niggles will have been removed. Life is so much more pleasant without totally unnecessary battles, confrontations, and shouting matches!

And when you're out, you're no longer waiting with a fast-beating heart for Something to Happen. You know now how to manage your walks so that Absolutely Nothing Happens!

Always look for a calm response from your dog. Always make distance - and don't worry, the distance will gradually close. After a while you will be hunting out those places you've always avoided, where you'll find dogs to practice! See what this terrier's owners said:

> "He is now able to look at other dogs and move away with us to continue his walk. This is a massive improvement in just a few weeks. It means that we no longer avoid dogs, but in fact go out looking for them so that we can work on his training."

Walking your dog is no longer a trial and a chore. Walking with your friend becomes a pleasure you look forward to. Remember the joy when you first got your dog? Keep in mind how she's a Brilliant Family Dog at home.

> "My dog is a great dog and becoming a great dog outdoors. I feel we've cracked most of what needs doing and her nervousness around other dogs is diminishing."

Before you leave, make sure you check out the Resources section - there's masses there to help you.

Any questions? You'll find me at beverley@brilliantfamilydog.com I'll usually reply within a couple of days. If you haven't heard from me in a week, write again. It means I was buried in email and your first one slipped down a crack.

And don't go without your free book!

Resources

You know now that there's light at the end of this tunnel! And to discover that the tunnel is much shorter than you think, get the next two parts of the puzzle here:

Essential Skills for your *Growly* but Brilliant Family Dog series
Book 1 **Why is my Dog so Growly?** *Teach your fearful, aggressive, or reactive dog confidence through understanding*
Book 2 **Change for your Growly Dog!** *Action steps to build confidence in your fearful, aggressive, or reactive dog*

For a very thorough, in-depth, approach, where I will be on hand to answer all your questions, go to

brilliantfamilydog.teachable.com

where you'll find info about the online course which takes all this to the next level, giving you personal support and encouragement as well as all the lessons and techniques you need to change your life with your Growly Dog.

For a free taster course: **www.brilliantfamilydog.com/growly**

And for loads of articles on Growly Dogs and Choice Training, go to **www.brilliantfamilydog.com** where you'll also find a course on solving everyday dog and puppy problems.

You'll also find the **Essential Skills for a Brilliant Family Dog** series of e-books helpful. Take a holistic view of your relationship with your dog and work on new skills inside the house as well as when you're out. If your dog has always had to be kept on lead because you were afraid he was not safe, you'll definitely need Book 4 for your new life!

Book 1 Calm Down! *Step-by-Step to a Calm, Relaxed, and Brilliant Family Dog*
Book 2 Leave it! *How to teach Amazing Impulse Control to your Brilliant Family Dog*
Book 3 Let's Go! *Enjoy Companionable Walks with your Brilliant Family Dog*
Book 4 Here Boy! *Step-by-step to a Stunning Recall from your Brilliant Family Dog*

And you'll be pleased to know that Book 1 is currently free at all e-book stores!

Here are the links to all the resources mentioned in this book:

Books by other authors:

Control Unleashed: Creating a Focused and Confident Dog by Leslie McDevitt, pub Clean Run Productions LLC, 2007 **http://controlunleashed.net/book.html**

Behavior Adjustment Training 2.0: New Practical Techniques for Fear, Frustration, and Aggression in Dogs by Grisha Stewart, pub Dogwise Publishing, 2016

Websites:
www.muzzleupproject.com - all things muzzle
www.goodfordogs.co.uk/products - Wiggles Wags and Whiskers Freedom Harness - UK and Europe [This is me. If you buy from me I will benefit financially, but it won't cost you any more.]
http://2houndswholesale.com/Where-to-Buy.html - Wiggles Wags and Whiskers Freedom Harness - rest of the world

http://youtu.be/_32dEnE7UIc - Lead-handling Techniques how-to video

https://www.youtube.com/watch?v=Mtn-BeI9lHE - *Pattern Games: Clicking for Confidence and Connection* by Leslie McDevitt, dvd 2011, Tawzer Dog LLC

http://www.melissaanddoug.com/product_list/1018276.1129966.3356 0.0.0/Dogs_%26amp%3B_Cats - wonderfully realistic stuffed dog and cat decoys

http://youtu.be/K9yOCb3rzOo Lacy works Look at That

1 yard = 0.9 metres

100 yards = 91 metres, much the same for our purposes

100 feet = 30 yards

Appreciation

I want to offer thanks to all those who have helped me get where I am in my life with dogs:

- First of all, my own long-suffering dogs! They have taught me so much when I've taken the time to listen.
- My reactive dog Lacy who is a star and has opened up a new world for me.
- My students, who have shown me how they learn best, enabling me to give them what they need to know in a way that works for them.
- Some legendary teachers, principal amongst them: Sue Ailsby, Leslie McDevitt, Grisha Stewart, Chirag Patel, Susan Garrett. I wholeheartedly recommend them. They are trailblazers.

Don't go without your free book!

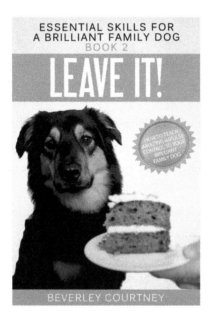

Impulse Control is particularly valuable for the reactive and anxious dog. Get a head start with your training by developing astonishing self-control in your dog! Change your dog from quick on the trigger, to thoughtful and reflective.

Go now and get your step-by-step book absolutely free at

Brilliant Family Dog

www.brilliantfamilydog.com/freebook-growly

About the author

I've been training dogs for many years. First for competitive dog sports and over time to be stellar family pets. For most of my life, I've lived with up to four dogs, so I'm well used to getting a multi-dog household to run smoothly. It soon became clear that a force-free approach was by far the most successful, effective, and rewarding for me and the dogs. I've done the necessary studying for my various qualifications - for rehab of anxious and fearful "aggressive" dogs, early puppy development, and learning theory and its practical applications. I am continually studying and learning this endlessly amazing subject!

There are some superb teachers and advocates of force-free dog training, and you'll find those I am particularly indebted to in the Appreciation Section. Some of the methods I show you are well-known in the force-free dog training community, while many have my own particular twist.

A lot of my learning has come through the Puppy Classes, Puppy Walks, and Growly Dog Courses I teach. These dog-owners are not looking for competition-standard training; they just want a Brilliant Family Dog they can take anywhere. It's a particular joy for me to see a Growly Dog who arrived at the first session a reactive bundle of nerves and fear, who ends up able to cope with almost anything the world chucks his way - becoming a relaxed and happy dog with a confident owner in the process.

Working with real dogs and their real owners keeps me humble - and resourceful! It's no good being brilliant at training dogs if you can't convey this enthusiasm and knowledge to the person the dog has to live with. So I'm grateful for everything my students have taught me about how they learn best.

Beverley Courtney BA(Hons) CBATI CAP2 MAPDT(UK) PPG
www.brilliantfamilydog.com

CPSIA information can be obtained
at www.ICGtesting.com
Printed in the USA
BVHW041946200420
577975BV00013B/1042